THE FECKIN'

BOOK OF EVERYTHING

IRISH

THE FECKIN'

BOOK OF EVERYTHING

IRISH

a gansey-load of deadly craic
for cute hoors and bowsies

COLIN MURPHY
AND DONAL O'DEA

FALL RIVER PRESS

New York

FALL RIVER PRESS

New York

An Imprint of Sterling Publishing Co., Inc.
1166 Avenue of the Americas
New York, NY 10036

This book contains portions from *Feckin' Book of Irish Songs, Feckin' Book of Irish Recipes, Feckin' Book of Irish Sayings, Feckin' Book of Irish Quotations, Feckin' Book of Irish Slang,* and *Feckin' Book of Irish Sex & Love* originally published by The O'Brien Press Ltd., 2004–2005.

This 2018 edition published by Fall River Press,
by arrangement with The O'Brien Press Ltd.

ISBN 978-1-4351-6732-2

For information about custom editions, special sales, and premium and corporate purchases, please contact Sterling Special Sales at 800-805-5489 or specialsales@sterlingpublishing.com.

Manufactured in the United States of America

2 4 6 8 10 9 7 5 3 1

sterlingpublishing.com

The quotes in this book have been drawn from many sources, and are assumed to be accurate as quoted in their previously published forms. Although every effort has been made to verify the quotes and sources, the publishers cannot guarantee their perfect accuracy.

Cover Design by David Ter-Avanesyan
Cover Images by Miceking/Shutterstock.com

contents

welcome to
Ireland, laddie

For anyone who claims to have even the tiniest drop of Irish blood flowing through their veins—and sure, don't we all, thank God—this book provides the ultimate collection of everything you'll need to take those final few steps into becoming a full-fledged, bona fide, 100-percent Irish person! There'll be shenanigans aplenty ahead as we take you on a no-holds-barred, laughter-filled tour of almost every nuance of Irish culture.

Discover how feckin' deadly (not to mention manky) Irish slang can be. Have a gander at some of these words and phrases and you'll soon realize precisely why they're gas craic altogether.

Take a peek under the skirts of sex and love in Ireland through the ages and find out about everything from Ireland's most lustful man to why clingfilm was a vital lovemaking accessory in Ireland in the seventies.

And of course, to really be in tune with what it is to be Irish, you have to know her music. You'll find the words to over twenty-five of the most famous and beloved songs, like "The Banks of My Own Lovely Lee," "Galway Bay," and "The Irish Rover," just to name a few. So the next time you hear "Danny Boy" being played, you won't have to stand there humming quietly to yourself in the corner…you can now sing along as badly as everyone else!

And finally, to further whet your appetite for learning about the wonders of Irish culture, we've included some of the most famous and delicious Irish recipes ever conceived. There's Dublin Coddle, Boxty, Colcannon, Fruit Brack, Bread Pudding, Black Velvet, and many more. And if any of this food makes you feel as rough as a bear's arse, you can go ahead and bite the back of my bollix.

So, whether you're a fine doorful of a woman or a man so mean you'd steal the sugar out of someone's tea, stop foostering about and get ready to reveal the inner Irish in you. You'd be a right eejit not to!

one

words and phrases

for when you go on the batter with a shower of savages

what did you say?

"Did you hear that the scrubber and the wagon were plastered last night and ended up in a mill? It was deadly!"

This sentence makes perfect sense to most Irish people. But to everyone else on the planet it means the following:

"Did you hear that the cleaning utensil and the four-wheeled, horse-drawn vehicle were covered in a lime/sand/water mixture and then transported to a processing factory? It had fatal consequences!"

This book sets out to avoid any such confusion arising in the future by explaining in clear and precise terms the meaning of a vast number of commonly used Irish slang words and expressions. If you, dear reader, believe that any of the listed phrases have been incorrectly translated, please feel free to go and ask my arse.

acting the maggot (expression)

Fooling about in a somewhat boisterous manner.
*(usage) "Anto! Will you stop acting de maggot
and give the oul' wan back her wheelchair."*

always a day late and
a pound short (expression)

Extremely unreliable. Prone to promise-breaking.
*(usage) The government is always a day late and
a pound short.*

are you headin'? (expression)
Are you about to depart?

arseways (adj)
Mishmash. Complete disarray. Total mess.
(usage) "Me car has been arseways since I ran over that pedestrian."

ask me arse (v)

(*see also* Gerrupdeyard!, Go and shite!)

What do you take me for, a silly billy?

(usage) "Lend YOU a fiver? Go and ask me arse!"

> The English have
> a miraculous power of
> turning wine into water.
>
> —Oscar Wilde
> *Poet and Dramatist*
> *(1854–1900)*

[i'd] ate a baby's arse through the bars of a cot (expression)

(*see also* Ate an oul' wan's arse through a blackthorn bush,
Ate the arse off a farmer through a tennis racquet)

I'm very hungry.

(usage) "Giving birth was so exhausting I could've ate a baby's arse through the bars of a cot."

[I'd] ate an oul' wan's arse through a blackthorn bush (expression)

(*see also* Ate a baby's arse through the bars of a cot, Ate the arse off a farmer through a tennis racquet)

I'm very hungry.

(*usage*) *"After drinking all that black stuff I'd ate an oul' wan's arse through a blackthorn bush!"*

[I'd] ate the arse off a farmer through a tennis racquet (expression)

(*see also* Ate a baby's arse through the bars of a cot, Ate an oul' wan's arse through a blackthorn bush)

I'm very hungry.

[I'd] ate the tyres off the truck that brought her knickers to the launderette (expression)

I find her extremely sexy.
(usage) "I'd ate the tyres off the truck that brought yer sister's knickers to the launderette."

> America is the only country that went from barbarism to decadence without civilization in between.
>
> —Oscar Wilde
> *Poet and Dramatist*
> *(1854–1900)*

away in the head (expression)
(*see also* Few brassers short of a whore house, Mentaller, Not the full shilling)
Insane. Not all there. (Northern Ireland)
(usage) Many Americans are away in the head.

BAð ðose (n)
Severe illness.

(usage) *"I'd a bad dose of the scutters after them ten pints of Guinness last night."*

BAGS (n)
(see also Hames)

A botched job.

(usage) *"The hairdresser made a right bags of me perm."*

BANG ON (adj)
Correct. Perfectly accurate.

(usage) *"That shot ye took at the ref's groin was bang on."*

BAnjaxeδ (adj)

(*see also* Knackered)

Broken. Severely damaged.

(usage) "*Me marriage to Deco is completely banjaxed.*"

> I often sit back and think, 'I wish I'd done that,' and find out later that I already have.
> —Richard Harris
> *Actor*
> *(1930–2002)*

Barrel (v)

Hurry. Race. Rush.

(usage) When the police arrived, the Minister for Justice barrelled out of the lap-dancing club.

[she's] bet down with a shovel (expression)

(*see also* Face like a full skip, Face like a pig licking piss off a nettle, Face like a smacked arse, Ganky, Head like a lump of wet turf, Wagon)

She's ugly. (Galway)

(*usage*) *"I think describing Lucy as 'having a head that looks bet down with a shovel' was being a bit too honest . . ."*

Better never than late.

—George Bernard Shaw
Dramatist
(1856–1950)

BIFFO (acronym)

(*see also* Bogtrotter, Culchie, Muck savage, Mulchie)

Big Ignorant Fecker From Offaly.

(*usage*) *"Em, excuse me BIFFO, would you mind not using the tablecloth as a hanky?"*

Bite the Back of my Bollix (expression)
Stop annoying me. Get lost.

Black Stuff (n)
Stout.

(usage) *"Nine pints of the black stuff and a gin and tonic for me mot, please."*

Blacker than the inside of a cow with its eyes closed and its tail down (expression)

Extremely dark (literally or figuratively).

(usage) "Ever since she realized she'd slept on me fish and chips her mood has been blacker than the inside of a cow with its eyes closed and its tail down."

Blarney (n)

(see also Oirish)

Nonsense talk used to charm foreigners.

(e.g.) "They say the ghost of Finn MacCumhall still stalks the Grand Canal. Buy another round and I'll tell you all about it, my American friend."

Blather (n) (v)

Empty, worthless talk.

(usage) "What are ye blatherin' on about, Taoiseach?"

BLATHER...BLATHER...

[like a] blue-arsed fly (expression)

Hectic. Busy.

(usage) "I was running around like a blue-arsed fly and I forgot to pick up Patrick from the pub, so he slept there."

bogtrotter (n)

(see also BIFFO, Culchie, Muck savage, Mulchie)

A person of rural extraction.

(usage) "And that, my bogtrotter friend, is what we call electricity."

bollix (n)

Extremely unpleasant man. Scrotum or testicles.

(usage) "That bollix is a pain in the bollix."

bollixed (adj)

(see also Fluthered, Gee-eyed, Langered, Ossified, Paralytic, Plastered, Rat-arsed)

Somewhat in excess of the legal alcohol driving limit.

(usage) "After twelve pints I was a bit bollixed."

BOWSIE (n)
Person (esp. male) of very disreputable character.
A useless good-for-nothing.
(usage) *"Is there anyone in the government who isn't a bleedin' bowsie?"*

BOXIN' the fox (expression)
Robbing an orchard.

BOYO (n)

Male juvenile (esp. delinquent).

(usage) "Y'know sarge, I think dem boyos outside the off-licence are up to no good with dem crobars and flick-knives."

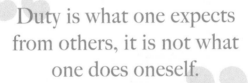

> Duty is what one expects from others, it is not what one does oneself.
>
> —Oscar Wilde
> *Poet and Dramatist*
> *(1854–1900)*

BRASSER (n)

A lady of the night.

(usage) "As a judge, it's my job to keep brassers like you off the street. So get into the bloody car!"

BREAKING ONE'S SHITE LAUGHING (expression)

Guffawing uncontrollably.

BRUTAL (adj)

Awful, terrible, hideous.

(usage) "The head on her was brutal."

bucketing down (expression)

Raining cats and dogs.

(usage) "Sure is bucketing down outside.
Might as well have another six pints."

bullin' (v)

Moaning. Complaining.

caught rapid (expression)

Caught in the act. Proven guilty beyond doubt.

(usage)"I was caught rapid in bed with me
mistress by me bit on the side."

chiseller (n)

Young child.

(usage) "That slapper's only eighteen and she's already had three chisellers."

circling over shannon (expression)

Drunk. (Derived from the visit of Boris Yeltsin.)

clatter (v) (n)

To slap playfully with palm.
(usage) "I only gave him one little clatter, yer Honour. His skull musta been brittle."

cmereawantcha (expression)

I would like to impart some news/information/gossip to you. (Cork)
(usage) "Cmereawantcha, I heard Patrick would get up on a cracked plate."

cod (v)

(see also Slag)

To pull one's leg in a jovial fashion.

I SENTENCE YOU TO 20 YEARS HARD LABOUR... NAH, ONLY CODDIN'! YOU'RE FINED €50.

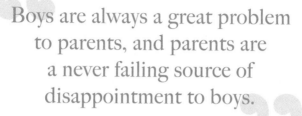

> Boys are always a great problem
> to parents, and parents are
> a never failing source of
> disappointment to boys.
>
> —James Connolly
> *Patriot and Socialist*
> *(1868–1916)*

come home with one arm as long as the other (expression)

Be unsuccessful in an enterprise.

(usage)

"I tried to get Mary to come home with me, but I just came home with one arm as long as the other."

(like a) constipated greyhound

(expression)

Down in the dumps. Depressed.

(like a) cow looking over a whitewashed wall (expression)

Wearing a vacant expression. Not too bright.

(usage) "The minister looks like a cow looking over a whitewashed wall."

CRAIC (n) *(Pronunciation: crack)*
Fun.
(usage) "There's great craic to be found in that pub on the corner."
Note: Misinterpretation of this expression has led to several arrests of foreign visitors who were caught trying to purchase a particular illicit drug.

> The wrong way always seems
> the more reasonable.

—George Moore
Writer
(1852–1933)

CULCHIE (n)
(see also BIFFO, Bogtrotter, Muck savage, Mulchie)
A person whose birthplace is beyond Dublin city limits.
(usage) Q: What d'ye call a culchie in a stretch Limo?
A: The deceased.

cute hoor (n)

Suspiciously resourceful gentleman.

(usage) Speaking from his yacht off Bermuda, the cute hoor denied he'd made any payments to politicians in return for favourable building contracts.

deadly (adj)

Great, brilliant, fantastic.

(usage) "Yer woman's got a deadly arse."

HE WAS DISTRACTED BY A GIRL'S ARSE AND DROVE OVER A CLIFF

NOW THATS WHAT I CALL DEADLY!

dense (adj)

(see also Thick)

Stupid.

(usage) "My accountant and solicitor say that paying tax is dense."

desperate (adj) *(Pronunciation: despera)*

Dreadful, awful.

(usage) "Yer man's arse is desperate after a few pints."

did you get your gee? (expression)

Did you have sex?

diddies (n)

(*see also* Knockers)

Extremely childish term for a woman's breasts.

(usage) "Counsel for the defence has got a magnificent pair of diddies, hasn't she m'Lud?"

[he] didn't have a bar in the grate (expression)

He was toothless.

(usage) "After old knuckler here had finished with him he didn't have a bar in the grate."

donkey's years (n)

Inordinately long time. An epoch. Time immemorial. *(e.g.) Period of time people of Ireland have been waiting for a National Soccer Stadium.*

National Stadium
Officially opened
2098 A.D.

[on the] doss (n)

(see also Hop, Mitch)

Failure to attend school/work during specified hours.

(usage) "I swear I wasn't on the doss. I really did have leukemia yesterday."

ᴅosseʀ (n)
Person with a relaxed attitude to attendance at his/her place of employment.
(e.g.) "Hey Mick, will ye move dis piano for me while I go an get me medicine in dat chemist, beside dat pub?"

ᴅʀawers (n)
Knickers. Panties.
(usage) "You could fit a hurling team into me wife's drawers. In fact I think she does on a regular basis."

ᴅʀy shite (n)
Someone of limited verbal/social skills.
(usage) "There was a dry shite on the seat beside me at the client party."

eat the head off (v)

To rebuke verbally in an aggressive manner.

(usage) "My bleedin' boyfriend eat the head off me just because I accidentally cut the TV cable during the World Cup final."

eccer (n)

Homework.

(usage) "Hey, Ma, do me eccer for me or I'll tell Da about the postman."

> **The Irish people do not gladly suffer common sense.**
>
> —Oliver St. John Gogarty
> *Poet and Essayist*
> *(1878–1957)*

eejit (n)

Person of limited mental capacity. Incapable fool. Complete moron. Imbecile.

(e.g.) Person(s) responsible for Ireland's health service.

effin' and blindin' (expression)
Swearing profusely.
(usage) "The Taoiseach was effin' and blindin' because the new government jet didn't have the Playboy channel."

eff off (v)
Restrained/polite swear word used in refined Irish society.
(usage) "Father, those chappies on the factory floor told me to 'eff off' when I inquired if they'd made my morning tea."

I SAY OLD SPORT, ANY CHANCE OF A QUICK EFF?

erection section (expression)

The slow set at a country dance.

[she has a] face like a full skip (expression)

(*see also* Bet down with a shovel, Face like a pig licking piss off a nettle, Face like a smacked arse, Ganky, Head like a lump of wet turf, Wagon)

She is ugly.

(*usage*) *"You don't have a face like a full skip . . . an empty skip, maybe."*

> Superstition is the religion
> of feeble minds.

—Edmund Burke
Lawyer, Writer, and Politician
(1729–1797)

[she has a] face like a pig licking
piss off a nettle (expression)
(*see also* Bet down with a shovel, Face like a full skip,
Face like a smacked arse, Ganky, Head like a lump of
wet turf, Wagon)
She is ugly.

[she has a] face like
a smacked arse (expression)
(*see also* Bet down with a shovel, Face like a full skip, Face like a pig licking piss off a nettle, Ganky, Head like a lump of wet turf, Wagon)
She is ugly.
(usage) "You idiot! You were supposed to operate on the cheeks of her arse. Now she has a face like a smacked arse."

> Ask me no questions, and
> I'll tell you no lies.
> —Oliver Goldsmith
> *Poet and Writer*
> *(1728–1774)*

fair play! (expression)
Well done!
(usage) "Fair play te ye for gettin' de leg over Deirdre."

fanny (n)

Female genitals.

(usage) "That Lucy's fanny was as tight as a camel's hole in a sand-storm."

Note: Some American visitors have inadvertently caused shock or offence through the mistaken belief that "fanny" refers to buttocks, as it does in the United States. For example, saying "After that bike ride, I feel like giving my fanny a good rub," may raise some eyebrows if spoken aloud in public.

feck (v) (n)

Politically correct term for f*ck.

(usage) "Ah, feck off Father Murphy. You're nothing but a feckin' fecker."

OH FECK,
I SAID
F*CK!!!

[a] few brassers short of a whorehouse (expression)

(*see also* Away in the head, Mentaller, Not the full shilling)
Crazy. Not fully sane.
(usage) *"Whoever decided to build the light rail system must be a few brassers short of a whorehouse."*

fierce (adj)

Very. Extremely.
(usage) *"I had a fierce bad headache after drinking Deirdre's perfume."*

EAU DE MISERY

fine bit of stuff (expression)

(*see also* Fine doorful of woman, Fine half alright,
Fine thing, Queer bit of skirt, Ride, Savage bit of arse)
Very attractive girl.
(usage) *"John's sister is a fine bit of stuff."*

fine doorful of a woman (expression)

(*see also* Fine bit of stuff, Fine half alright, Fine thing, Queer bit of skirt, Ride, Savage bit of arse)

A fine strapping lass.

(*usage*) *"I can't wait until she grows up to be a fine doorful of a woman."*

[a] fine half alright (expression)

(*see also* Fine bit of stuff, Fine doorful of woman, Fine thing, Queer bit of skirt, Ride, Savage bit of arse)

A very attractive girl. (Cork)

(*usage*) *"She's a fine half alright—actually two fine halfs if you ask me."*

ꜰɪɴe ᴛʜɪɴɢ (n)

(*see also* Fine bit of stuff, Fine doorful of woman, Fine half alright, Queer bit of skirt, Ride, Savage bit of arse)
An attractive man or woman.
(usage) "She looks like a fine thing after seven pints."

> Life for a GAA player isn't
> all beer and football.
> Some of us haven't touched
> a football in months.
> —A Kerry Inter-County Footballer
> *(1984)*

ꜰʟaʜᴜʟaᴄʜ (adj) *(Pronunciation: Flah-hule-uck)*

Generous.
(usage) The councillor was feeling flahulach after he got his bribe from the property developer.

fluthered (adj)

(see also Bollixed, Gee-eyed, Langered, Ossified, Paralytic, Plastered, Rat-arsed)

Having a high blood-alcohol ratio.

(usage) "I was so fluthered last night I slept with the missus."

fooster (v)

Not getting much done. Fiddling about.

(usage) "Will ye stop foosterin' about Mick and stamp on the goalie's face!"

Gaa (n)

Sport played by the GAA (Gaelic Athletic Association).

(usage) "Gaa is a great game. It's just a shame about the GAA."

Gaff (n)

Home. Place of residence.

(usage) "Dat's some gaff yer woman de President has in de Phoenix Park."

> **To** many, no doubt,
> he will seem blatant and bumptious,
> but we prefer to regard him
> as being simply British.

—Oscar Wilde
Poet and Dramatist
(1854–1900)

Gammy (adj)

Damaged. Crooked. Useless.

(usage) The entire cabinet is gammy.

Ganky (adj)

(*see also* Bet down with a shovel, Face like a full skip, Face like a pig licking piss off a nettle, Face like a smacked arse, Head like a lump of wet turf, Wagon)

Repulsive. Ugly.

(*usage*) *Q: What's the difference between a ganky-looking girl and an absolute ride?*
A: About ten pints!

Gansey-load (adj)

NOW THAT'S WHAT I CALL A GANSEY-LOAD!

(*see also* Rake of)

Many. Lots. An excess.

(*usage*) *"There's a gansey-load of dossers in the Dáil."*

Gargle (n) (v)

Drink (alcohol).

(*usage*) *The cabinet single-handedly prevented the closure of the brewery by retiring to the Dáil bar for a "gargle or two."*

GAS (adj)
Amusing. Funny. Hilarious.
(usage) *"It was gas when Cormac broke his collar-bone."*

GEE (n)
Female reproductive organ.
(usage) *"I've a pain in me gee trying to get laid tonight."*

GEEBAG (n)
Woman of unpleasant character.
(usage) *"Me wife's a right geebag."*

gee-eyed (adj)
(*see also* Bollixed, Fluthered, Langered, Ossified, Paralytic, Plastered, Rat-arsed)

Having partaken of a large quantity of ale and/or spirits.

(*e.g.*) *Subject was so inebriated that his eyes have shifted from the normal horizontal orientation.*

gerrupdeyard! (expression)
(*see also* Ask me arse, Go and Shite!)

Get lost.

get off with (v)

Be successful with a romantic advance.

YER WOMAN GOT ON THE BUS WITH THE GOALIE BUT SHE GOT OFF WITH THE WHOLE TEAM

DOLLYMOUNT F.C.

[he'd] get up on a cracked plate (expression)

He's desperate for sex.

(usage) "That Mick is so manky, he'd get up on a cracked plate."

[she'd] get up on a stiff BREEZE (expression)

She's easily sexually aroused.

(usage) "They say she'd get up on a stiff breeze, but I wouldn't mind putting the wind up her myself."

Go and shite! (expression)

(see also Ask me arse, Gerrupdeyard!)

I am not in agreement with your suggestion.

(usage) "The priest told me to abstain from bad language, so I told him to go and shite!"

> **The march of the human mind is slow.**
>
> —Edmund Burke
> *Philosopher*
> *(1729–1797)*

GOBDAW (n)

(see also Gobshite)

Person of restricted mental ability.

(usage) "The Minister for Finance is a complete gobdaw."

GOBSHITE (n)
(*see also* Gobdaw)
Person of below average IQ. Socially inept individual.
(*usage*) *"The Minister for Finance is a complete gobshite."*

GOING NINETY TO THE DOZEN (expression)
Going very fast.
(*usage*) *"According to my speed camera, you were going ninety to the dozen, boyo."*

GOLLIER (n)
A mass of phlegm expelled from the mouth at high speed.
(*usage*) *"I landed a gollier in the geography teacher's coffee."*

GOMBEEN MAN (n)
Petty, snivelling, fawning underling.
(e.g.) Chief executive of any Irish semi-state company.

GO ON THE BATTER (expression)
Go out for an evening of excessive drinking.
(usage) "My girlfriend goes on the batter more often than I do."

GO WAY OUTTA THAT! (expression)
That's unbelievable.

GOUGER (n)
(*see also* Sleeveen)
Aggressive, repulsive person.
*(usage) "Do you really take this gouger
to be your lawful wedded husband?"*

> I was elected by
> the women of Ireland,
> who instead of rocking the cradle,
> rocked the system.
> —Mary Robinson
> *Irish President*
> *(b.1944)*

GUFF (n)
Feeble excuses. Blatant lies.
*(e.g.) "Sorry I'm late, boss. I had to take me Ma to
the hospital for her spine replacement operation."*

GURRIER (n)

Hooligan. Delinquent. Ruffian.

*(usage) "Give the oul' lad back
his teeth, ye little gurrier!"*

hames (n)

(see also Bags)

Complete mess.

*(usage) "The plastic surgeon
made a hames of me arse."*

has a great lip for the stout (expression)

Indulges in alcohol. (Cork)

*(usage) "My granddad always said I'd inherit his
great lip for the stout."*

have a great time for (expression)

To like a lot (esp. a person).

*(usage) "I've always had a great time for Mary's
diddies."*

haven't got a baldy (expression)
Have no chance.

[i'd] have to be dug out of her (expression)
(see also Leave it rot in her)
I find her highly arousing.
(usage) "You might have to be dug out of her, but I'd prefer to be buried in her."

[she has a] head like a lump of wet turf (expression)

(*see also* Bet down with a shovel, Face like a full skip, Face like a pig licking piss off a nettle, Face like a smacked arse, Ganky, Wagon)

She is ugly.

(*usage*) *"Yer cousin has a head like a lump of wet turf when she gets out of the water."*

head-the-ball (n)

Term of address: "you."

heavin' (adj)

(*see also* Jammers)

Thoroughly packed.

(*usage*) *"In the planning trial the defendant's box was heavin' with county councillors."*

> Everybody sets out to do something, and everybody does something, but no one does what he sets out to do.
> —George Moore
> *Writer*
> *(1852–1933)*

hockeyed (v)

Heavily defeated.

(*usage*) *"Ireland hockeyed Brazil five-nil in the World Cup final, and then me bleedin' missus woke me up."*

hold yer whist (expression)
Wait a minute. Be quiet.
(usage) "I wish the president would hold his whist."

hole (n)
Anus.
(usage) "Piles are a pain in the hole."

holy joe (n)
Self-righteous, sanctimonious hypocrite.
(usage) If Holy Joes are so holy, how come there's always so many of them queuing for confession?

holy show (expression)
Disgrace. Spectacle.
(usage) "Me Ma made a holy show of herself when she dropped her pint into the baptismal font."

PLEASE GOD, CAN THERE BE WORLD PEACE AND CAN I HAVE A NEW CAR

hooley (n)

Raucous celebration involving drinking and singing.
(usage) "... and folks, I'm asked to invite you all to a hooley in Murphy's pub immediately after Mick's funeral."

> I blew hundreds of thousands of pounds on women and drinking—the rest I just squandered.
>
> —George Best
> *Footballer*
> *(b.1946)*

hop (v)

(see also Doss, Mitch)
Play truant from school.
(usage) "Let's go on the hop and get pissed. I'm fed up teaching those bleedin' kids anyway."

horse it into ye (expression)
Consume alcohol/food rapidly.
(usage) "You'll have to horse it into ye if ye want to get langered before yer wife gets home."

howaya (greeting)
Hello. Hi.
(usage) "Howaya, ye big bollix!"

how's about ye? (greeting)
Hello. How are you? (Northern Ireland)
(usage) "When he said 'How's about ye, beautiful' I said 'How's about ye get lost?'"

how's it goin', head? (expression)
(see also How's it hanging, boy?, How's she cuttin'?, How's the craic?)
How are things with you? (Dublin)
(usage) "How's it goin', knockers—I mean, head?"

how's it hanging, boy? (expression)

(*see also* How's it goin', head?, How's she cuttin'?,
How's the craic?)

How are things with you? (Cork)

how's she cuttin'? (expression)

(*see also* How's it goin', head?, How's it hanging, boy?,
How's the craic?)

How is life, my good friend?

(usage) "How's she cuttin', yer honour?"

> Friendship is one
> of the most tangible things
> in a world which offers fewer
> and fewer supports.

—Kenneth Branagh
Actor
(b.1960)

how's the craic? (expression)

(*see also* How's it goin', head?, How's it hanging, boy?,
How's she cuttin'?)
How are you? What's happening?
(*usage*) *"How's the craic, Deirdre?"*

how's the form? (expression)

How are you feeling?
(*usage*) *"How's the form? I hear that's the hardest
part when you apply for a mortgage."*

how's the talent? (expression)
Are there any attractive females/males present?

I am in me wick (expression)
I certainly am not!

(usage) *"She asked me if I was sober and I said 'I am in me wick!'"*

If he went to a wedding, he'd stay for the christening (expression)

He always overstays his welcome.

I will in me arse/bollix/hole/fanny (expression)

I absolutely refuse to do what you suggest.

(usage) "Marry you? I will in me bollix!"

Jackeen (n)

A rural person's derogatory name for a Dubliner.
(usage) Q: What does a Jackeen say on his first day at work?
A: What do I do now, Daddy?

Jacks (n)

Toilet, restroom.
(usage) "Ye tink dat's bad? Wait 'til ye see de state of de jacks in de Dáil."

Jammers (adj)

(see also Heavin')
Extremely crowded.
(usage) "The Dáil bar is permanently jammers."

Jammy (adj)

Exceedingly lucky.
(usage) "The jammy bastard won the Lotto again."

Janey mack! (expression)

(*see also* Stop the lights!)

Expression of utter disbelief. Wow!

(usage) "Janey Mack! That politician told the truth!"

> "God created alcohol so that people who looked like me could get laid as well."
> —Sinead Murphy
> *Irish Writer*
> *(b.1959)*

Jar (n)

Pint of beer or stout.

(usage) "I'm dying for a jar. The court will adjourn until 2 p.m."

Jaysus! (expression)

Jesus Christ!

(usage) "Ah Jaysus, ye puked in me pint!"

jo maxi (n)

Taxi. Cab.

(usage) "Eh, hello. I'd like a Jo Maxi please to collect four people from Madame Le Whip's Maison de Plaisir and take us back to Government Buildings."

joe soap (n)

Anybody.
Somebody.
Nondescript person.
(usage) "I shagged some Joe Soap last night."

WHAT ARE YOU GOING TO CALL HIM, MRS SOAP?

JOE!

kip (n)

A place/establishment of poor repute. A dump.
(usage) "Benidorm is a kip."

knackered (adj)

(*see also* Banjaxed, Shattered, Wrecked)

Very tired. Broken beyond repair.

(usage) "My arse was knackered after that vindaloo."

SO YOU'VE FINALLY HAD THE JOB DONE ON YOUR KNOCKERS

YEAH, I HAD THEM REDUCED.

knockers (n)

(*see also* Diddies)

Mammaries. Breasts.

(usage) "Are dem knockers real, missus?"

langer (n)

Male reproductive organ.

(usage) Countrywoman A: This carrot reminds me of me husband's langer.

Countrywoman B: Ye mean the size of it?

Countrywoman A: No. The dirt of it.

langered (adj)

(*see also* Bollixed, Fluthered, Gee-eyed, Ossified, Paralytic, Plastered, Rat-arsed)

Very drunk.

(usage) *"I was so langered I woke up with a kebab in me knickers."*

> It has been scientifically proven that people who don't drink and don't smoke live longer—and it serves them right!
>
> —Moss Keane
> *Irish International Rugby Player*
> *(b. 1948)*

lash (v)

To rain heavily.

(usage) *"We had two weeks' holiday in the sunny southeast and it never stopped bleedin' lashin'."*

[I'D] leave it rot in her (expression)

(*see also* Have to be dug out of her)

I think she's exceedingly sexy.

leg it (v)

To flee rapidly. To run away.

(*usage*) "Let's leg it before the waiter comes back with the bill, Sarge."

[he'd] lick drink off a scabby leg (expression)

He's very fond of alcoholic beverages.

[he'd] light a smoke in his pocket (expression)

(*see also* Steal the sugar out of your tea, Tight as a camel's arse in a sandstorm)

He's extremely mean.

(*usage*) "*He'd light a smoke in his pocket before giving someone a cigarette.*"

loaf (v)

To head-butt.

(usage) "Righ', Murphy. As a bouncer, your primary job is to loaf everyone who tries to get into this bleedin' nightclub."

> "Trousers may now be worn
> by lady members on the course
> but must be removed
> when entering the clubhouse."
> —Sign at a Well-Known Irish Golf Club

lob it into me, boss (expression)

Give me alcohol quickly.

(usage) "Lob it into me, boss, and then I'll give you the rest of this paperwork."

lookin' for a dig in the snot locker? (expression)

I am about to beat you senseless.

(usage) "When you have an upturned nose like that you're just lookin' for a dig in the snot locker."

> This is one race of people for whom psychoanalysis is of no use whatsoever.
>
> —Sigmund Freud (about the Irish)
> *Psychoanalyst*
> *(1856–1939)*

manky (adj)

Disgustingly filthy.

(e.g.) Any street, waterway, public toilet, or beauty spot in Ireland.

massive (adj)

(see also Rapid)

Great. Fantastic.

(usage) "Look at the tiny little arse on yer woman. It's massive!"

mentaller (n)

(*see also* Away in the head, Few brassers short of a whore house, Not the full shilling)

Nut case. Looney.

(*usage*) *Politician: Commissioner, about a thousand of the Gardai are complete mentallers!*
Commissioner: I know, it's just not enough, is it?

me oul' segotia (expression)

Term of endearment. My old flower.

(*usage*) *"Any chance of a ride, me oul' segotia?"*

> " **True friends stab you in the front.** "
>
> —Oscar Wilde
> *Poet and Dramatist*
> *(1854–1900)*

mill (n) (v)

Fight. Public brawl.

(*usage*) *"Hey, look lads! A mill between wimmin!"*

mind yer house! (expression)

Watch your back! Look behind you.
(Northern Ireland)
*(usage) "Karen told me to my mind my house
just before that bowsie smacked me arse."*

miss by a gee hair (expression)

(see also Miss by a gnat's gonad)
Miss by a very narrow margin.

miss by a gnat's gonad (expression)

(*see also* Miss by a gee hair)

Miss by a very narrow margin.

(*usage*) *"I missed the goal by a gnat's gonad
and hit the goalie's gonads instead."*

mitch (v)

(*see also*
Doss, Hop)

To play truant.
To skip school.

(*usage*)

DON'T WORRY BARMAN, OF COURSE
WE'RE OVER 18!

*"Honest, we're not mitchin', Guard.
We're doin' a project on
juvenile alcohol consumption."*

mot (n)

Girlfriend.

(*usage*) *"Me mot drinks tequila sunrises
like there's no tomorrow."*

[the] mot's crossbar (expression)
State of male arousal.

muck savage (n)
(*see also* BIFFO, Bogtrotter, Culchie, Mulchie)
Country fellow lacking in sophistication.
*(usage) "No, you big muck savage, you may not
eat curry chips in the delivery room."*

mulchie (n)

(see also BIFFO, Bogtrotter,
Culchie, Muck savage)
Person from a small
rural town.
(usage) *"That, my
mulchie friend, is a
three-story building."*

BE THE HOKEY, WOULDYA
LOOK AT THE SIZE OF THAT.

murder (adj)

Very difficult. Almost impossible.
(usage) *"Getting a Cavan man to buy his round
is murder."*

my mouth is as dry
as an arab's tackie (expression)

I'm extremely thirsty (esp. because of a
hangover). (Limerick)
(usage) *"I was so ossified last night I don't know
how I ended up in this desert, but my mouth is as
dry as an Arab's tackie."*

[in the] nip (adj)
Nude. Naked.
(usage) "The doctor examined me in the nip. Whatever happened to his clothes is anyone's guess."

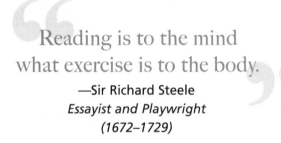

> **Reading is to the mind what exercise is to the body.**
> —Sir Richard Steele
> *Essayist and Playwright*
> *(1672–1729)*

nixer (n)
Job done on the side, for cash, thus avoiding tax.
(usage) "Tell you what, I'll write your next speech as a nixer, Minister."

not the full shilling (adj)

(*see also* Away in the head, Few brassers short of a whore house, Mentaller)

Mentally challenged. Not fully sane. Nuts.

(e.g.) Anyone who attempts to commute by means of public transport in Dublin or Cork on a regular basis.

off me face (expression)

Inebriated.

oul' fella (n)

Father.

(usage) "Me oul' fella hasn't been seen since six o'clock last night when he went to the pub."

oul' wan (n)

Mother.

(usage) "Me oul' wan had me when she was sixteen."

oirish (n)

(see also Blarney)

Mythical language and culture used by Americans and British when portraying Irish people.

(e.g.) "Top o' de mornin' te ye, be de hokey. D'ye happen te know, me good sir, where I'd be findin' a leprechaun dis fine day, at all, at all?"

> ❝There is none so blind
> as they that will not see.❞
> —Jonathan Swift
> *Author and Dean of St. Patrick's Cathedral*
> *(1667–1745)*

OSSIFIED (adj)
(*see also* Bollixed, Fluthered, Gee-eyed, Langered, Paralytic,
Plastered, Rat-arsed)
Totally inebriated.
*(usage) "Do you know it takes just three pints
to get an Englishman ossified?"*

THREE PINTS OF GUINNESS AND A SICK
BUCKET FOR MY ENGLISH FRIEND.

[she has a] pair of puppies playing in her blouse (expression)

She is a braless, big-bosomed girl.

WHAT DO YOU THINK OF MY PUPPIES?

VERY CUDDLY. AND THEY SEEM TO GET BIGGER EVERY TIME I SEE THEM.

paralytic (adj)

(*see also* Bollixed, Fluthered, Gee-eyed, Langered, Ossified, Plastered, Rat-arsed)

So inebriated one actually passes out.

(usage) "Do you know that it takes just four pints to get an Englishman paralytic?"

piss-up (n)

Night of revelry and imbibing alcohol.

(usage) *"I must interrupt counsel's lengthy summation to remind him that the barristers' annual piss-up starts at five."*

[this] place is a sword fight (expression)

There are too many males present.

plastered (adj)
(*see also* Bollixed, Fluthered, Gee-eyed, Langered, Ossified, Paralytic, Rat-arsed)
Very drunk.
(usage) "I was so plastered that the taxi driver actually made sense."

> In 1969 I gave up women and alcohol, and it was the worst twenty minutes of my life.
> —George Best
> *Footballer*
> *(b.1946)*

puss (n)
Sulky face.
(usage) "Frank had a puss on him just because me and the girls were watching Emmerdale *during the World Cup final."*

[he'd] put the heart crossways in you (expression)

He'd make you extremely fearful.

put the mockers on (expression)

Put a hex on.

(usage) "When he wouldn't go out with me I put the mockers on him and made him kiss a pig."

queer bit of skirt (expression)

(*see also* Fine bit of stuff, Fine doorful of woman, Fine half
alright, Fine thing, Ride, Savage bit of arse)

A very sexy girl.

rake of (adj)

(*see also* Gansey-load)

A lot of. Many.

(*usage*) *"We've got a rake of ideas for ripping
off tourists."*

Rapid (adj)

(*see also* Massive)

Great. Fantastic. Amazing.

(usage) "Yer mot's knockers are rapid."

> " Work is the curse of
> the drinking classes. "
>
> —Oscar Wilde
> *Poet and Dramatist*
> *(1854–1900)*

Rat-arsed (adj)

(*see also* Bollixed, Fluthered, Gee-eyed, Langered, Ossified, Paralytic, Plastered)

Very drunk.

(usage) "I was so rat-arsed I ate a spice-burger."

REDDNER (n)
Blush.

(usage) *"I'll tell ye, Mary, it was so small he had a reddner."*

RIDE (n) (v)
(see also Fine bit of stuff, Fine doorful of woman, Fine half alright, Fine thing, Queer bit of skirt, Savage bit of arse, Shag)

An attractive female or male (n).

To partake in sexual intercourse (v).

(usage) *"I had a ride of that ride in accounts."*

ROMAN HANDS AND RUSSIAN FINGERS
(expression)

(Of) a man who gropes women.

(usage) *"It was bad enough that he had Roman hands and Russian fingers, but then he insisted we go Dutch."*

[as] ROUGH as a BEAR'S ARSE (expression)
Extremely hungover. Unwell.

SAVAGE BIT OF ARSE (expression)
(*see also* Fine bit of stuff, Fine doorful of woman, Fine half alright, Fine thing, Queer bit of skirt, Ride)
A very attractive girl.
(*usage*) *"My new girlfriend is a savage bit of arse."*

SCANGER (n)

(*see also* Scrubber, Slapper)

Female lacking in sophistication.

(usage) "The scanger drank her finger bowl."

[AS] SCARCE AS hen's teeth (expression)

(*see also* Scarce as shite from a rocking horse)

Extremely scarce. Nonexistent.

[as] scarce as shite from a rocking horse (expression)

(*see also* Scarce as hen's teeth)

In extremely short supply. Nonexistent.

(*usage*) *"The money that comes in from this toy store is as scarce as shite from a rocking horse."*

scratcher (n)

Bed.

(*usage*) *"If you're not out of the scratcher and here in ten minutes operating on this man's brain, you're fired."*

scrubber (n)

(*see also* Scanger, Slapper)

Woman of low moral fiber and little sophistication.

(*usage*) *"She's such a scrubber that she smokes during oral sex."*

scutters (n)
Diarrhea.
(usage) "Eight pints of Harp and a curry always gives my missus the scutters."

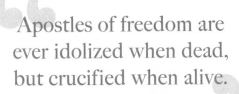

Apostles of freedom are
ever idolized when dead,
but crucified when alive.

—James Connolly
Patriot and Socialist
(1868–1916)

shag (v)
(see also Ride)
To have sexual intercourse.
(usage) "That Viagra is great shaggin' stuff."

shattered (adj)

(*see also* Knackered, Wrecked)

Very tired. Requiring sleep.

(usage) "Listen, Taoiseach. The whole cabinet's been working for nearly an hour and we're all shattered."

shenanigans (n)

Mischievous, suspicious, underhand, devious goings-on.

(usage) "Next item on today's county council agenda: planning shenanigans. Sorry, uh, planning submissions."

shite (adj)

Of extraordinarily poor quality.

(usage) The health service is shite.

shite hawk (n)

Swine. Pig. Scumbag.

(usage) "When I asked that shite hawk Sean what we'd use for protection he said we could use de bus shelter."

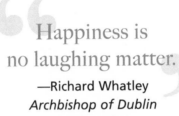

> Happiness is no laughing matter.
> —Richard Whatley
> *Archbishop of Dublin*
> *(1787–1863)*

shower of savages (expression)

Loud, ignorant, unsophisticated crowd of people.

(usage) Q: Who's that shower of savages in the corner?

A: That's the cabinet.

[I'm as] sick as a plane to Lourdes (expression)

I am feeling very poorly.

single (n)

Bag of chips.

(usage) "Micko was so good in bed I nearly dropped me single."

SKIVER (n)

Person who avoids honest work.

(usage) Kid: When I grow up I want to be a skiver like you, Dad.

Dad: So you want to work in the insurance industry, then?

> **She wears her clothes as if they were thrown on with a pitchfork.**
> —Jonathan Swift
> *Author and Dean of St. Patrick's Cathedral (1667–1745)*

SLAG (v)

(see also Cod)

Make fun of a person in a lighthearted, friendly manner.

(e.g.) "Yer a big ignorant sleeven of a muck savage, ye thick bogtrotter ye."

slapper (n)

(*see also* Scanger, Scrubber)

Female of low morals and poor taste in clothing.

(usage) "You're not really going to make that slapper a minister, are you, Taoiseach?"

slash (n) (v)

Urination.

(usage) ". . . if I may interrupt my learned friend, m'Lud, as I'm dying for a slash."

sleeveen (n)

(*see also* Gouger)

Devious, sly, repulsive individual.

(e.g.) Any member of Ireland's car insurance industry.

[as] small as a mouse's tit (expression)

Tiny. Microscopic.

(usage) "Her diddies were as small as a mouse's tit."

soften his cough (expression)

Teach him a lesson. (Cork)

so 'n' so (n)

Disreputable person.

(usage) "So 'n' so is only so-so in bed."

sound as a pound (expression)

Very reliable.

(usage) "Never mind that noise sir, this car is sound as a pound."

spondulicks (n)
Money.

(usage) *"Wait'll ye see the spondulicks our insurance company screwed out of Irish drivers last year."*

stall the ball there (expression)
Wait a second.

(usage) *"Stall the ball there for a minute lads . . . yes luv, I'll get some washing powder on the way home . . ."*

[he'd] steal the sugar out of your tea (expression)
(see also Light a smoke in his pocket, Tight as a camel's arse in a sandstorm)

He's extremely mean.

(usage) *"I was so poor I had to steal sugar out of people's tea and everyone thought I did it just to be mean."*

stop the lights! (expression)

(*see also* Janey mack!)

Exclamation of disbelief. Wow!

(now yer) suckin' diesel (expression)

Now you're talking! Now you're doing well!

(*usage*) *"Increase car insurance premiums by 20 percent for no reason? Now yer suckin' diesel, Mr. Chief Executive!"*

thick (adj)

(*see also* Dense)

Extremely stupid.

(*e.g.*) *The person who conceived RTÉ's Angelus slot.*

There is no sin except stupidity.

—Oscar Wilde
Poet and Dramatist
(1854–1900)

[as] thick as a cow's arse (expression)

(*see also* Thick as Pig Shite)

Really stupid.

(*usage*) *"He tried to milk a bull. He's as thick as a cow's arse."*

[as] thick as pig shite (expression)

(*see also* Thick as a cow's arse)

Excessively stupid.

(*usage*) *Tourists are as thick as pig shite.*

throw shapes (v)

To swagger excessively. To show off.

(usage) *"Will you stop throwing shapes at those slappers or we'll never get a bleedin' shag."*

[as] tight as a camel's arse in a sandstorm (expression)

(see also Light a smoke in his pocket, Steal the sugar out of your tea)

Very mean.

(e.g.) *"We have to repossess your one room slum. Alleyed Bank of Erin's profits were down to 3 billion last year."*

[she has a] tongue that would clip a hedge (expression)

She can be very direct/hurtful.

(e.g.) *"Your langer looks like half a banana."*

two sockets and no plug (expression)
Two lesbians.

up the pole (expression)
With child. Pregnant.
(usage) *"Great news, Ma, I'm up de pole. I mean, eh, engaged."*

up to ninety (expression)
Really busy.

(as) useful as a cigarette lighter on a motorbike (expression)
(*see also* Useful as a lighthouse on a bog, Useful as tits on a bull)
Totally useless.
(*usage*) *"I had to fire him for being as useful as a cigarette lighter on a motorbike."*

[as] useful as a lighthouse on a bog (expression)

(*see also* Useful as a cigarette lighter on a motorbike, Useful as tits on a bull)

Totally useless.

(usage) *"That invention is as useful as a lighthouse on a bog."*

> "Necessity, the mother of invention."
>
> —George Farquhar
> *Poet and Dramatist*
> *(1678–1707)*

[as] useful as tits on a bull (expression)

(*see also* Useful as a cigarette lighter on a motorbike, Useful as a lighthouse on a bog)

Totally useless.

(usage) *"Patty won't let me touch 'em at all. She's about as useful as tits on a bull."*

wagon (n)

(*see also* Bet down with a shovel, Face like a full skip, Face like a pig licking piss off a nettle, Face like a smacked arse, Ganky, Head like a lump of wet turf)

Unattractive female.

(usage) *"Better gimme another pint. She still looks like a wagon."*

what are ye at? (expression)

What are you doing? (Northern Ireland)

wind your neck down (expression)

Wise up! (Northern Ireland)

(usage) "Wind your neck down and look me in the eyes."

wojus (adj)

Extremely poor quality.

(usage) "Every bleedin' government service in Ireland is wojus."

[he] wouldn't work to warm himself (expression)

He's really lazy.

wrecked (adj)

(*see also* Knackered, Shattered)

Extremely tired. Worn out.

(usage) Ex-Civil Servant: I'm wrecked doing this . . .
what d'ye call it?

Private Employee: Work.

ye buck eejit ye (expression)

You idiot. (Northern Ireland)

YER WAN (n)

Female whose name escapes one.

Nondescript individual.

(usage) "Yer wan over there. Yeah, her. Me wife."

> *One of the worst things that can happen in life is to win a bet on a horse at an early age.*
>
> —Danny McGoorty
> *Irish-American Pool Player*
> *(1901–1970)*

YOU'RE WHA? (expression)

Alleged method of proposing to one's sweetheart on Dublin's north side.

(usage) "You're bleedin' wha?"

two

a guide to sex and love

that's not fit for dacent people's eyes

looking for a shag?

Adultery, massage parlours, lustful thoughts, confession, Viagra, lap dancing . . . here in one uncensored chapter is everything you ever wanted to know about sex and love in Ireland past and present. And what a sordid tale awaits you!

Find out who shouldn't have, but did; why there were plenty of "Fallen Women" but no "Fallen Men"; learn about the seventh century version of the one night stand; discover who was famous for her "willing thighs"; and find out about the extreme measures taken to prevent unfortunate Irish people from thinking about their wobbly bits and return to singing songs about the Great Famine or the 1916 Rising.

It's the sex education that the Irish never got at school! So dim the lights, snuggle up to your partner, and let us slowly strip bare the subject of sex and love in the Emerald Isle. By the end, you'll be gasping for more . . .

abstinence from sex: This will make you a better person. At least that's what the Church has been trying to beat into us since ancient times. The bishops really got stuck on the "no sex please, we're Irish" thing around the seventh century, beginning with their own priests, most of whom were married. One decree banned sex on so many occasions (Lent, Advent, Sundays, the day the bin-man came, etc.) that opportunities for a quick grope were limited to five minutes on a Tuesday afternoon in August.

adultery: Adultery is, of course, a sin. And in the eyes of the Irish Catholic church, looking at one's wife lustfully is also a form of adultery. So, if you want to make love to your wife after you've had some Chinese takeaway and bottle of red, you should go around blindfolded for several hours beforehand. This may make trimming the hedge or fixing the kitchen shelf a little tricky, but at least you can enjoy your semi-drunken tumble without a mark on your soul, although your body may look like it's been through a meat grinder.

agony aunts: Typical question to an Irish agony aunt, or advice columnist, in the 1960s to 1980s: "If a boy squeezes my breast will I become pregnant?" Typical answer: "No, but breast squeezing is a sin anyway, whether you're the squeezer or the squeezee. Go to confession and don't do it again." Among the foremost dispensers of coy advice on our love lives were Angela McNamara and Frankie Byrne. When the phenomenon of the ultra conservative agony aunt disappeared, it solved a lot of problems.

> "Pity those who nature abuses;
> never those who abuse nature."
> —Richard Brinsley Sheridan
> *Playwright*
> *(1751–1816)*

archbishop john charles mcquaid: From 1940 to 1972, the Archbishop directed the course of the nation in issues of morality, and for

his purposes this meant everything. It even included forbidding the importation of tampons, as they might make women excited! Considering that Dev actually got this guy to approve the 1937 Constitution before showing it to the cabinet, it's probably not surprising how sexually screwed up we were as a nation for the next half century or so. (For issues upon which he had a direct influence see also Abstinence, Adultery, Celibacy, Censorship, Contrac . . . ah, what the hell, see the whole damn chapter!)

Bachelor festivals: The Ballybunion and Mullingar Bachelor Festivals offer the opportunity for eligible bachelors to make eejits of themselves in front of hordes of women, who get to holler obscenities just like men. The winner, one assumes, can expect to be ineligible for next year's competition. In the 1970s the Ballybunion event was misleadingly called The Gay Bachelor Festival—gay in those days implying jolly and

carefree. The "Gay" bit was dropped, presumably after a few of the candidates displayed a distinct lack of interest in girls.

Bishop Eamonn Casey:

After centuries of sexual repression, the dam finally burst in 1992. And we owe it all to Eamo. Never shy to denounce the evils of premarital sex, it turned out that the bold bishop had had a booboo or two of his own in this regard, literally. Luckily, he was caught by the short and curlies, and the

ERECTED
IN HONOUR
OF BISHOP
EAMONN CASEY

rejection of the Church's teachings on sex has been snowballing ever since. For this we owe Bishop Casey a large debt of gratitude, and he deserves a huge erection (of a statue) in his honour.

> **Forgive your enemies, but never forget their names.**
> —John Fitzgerald Kennedy
> *U.S. President*
> *(1917–1963)*

BOOK BANS: Between the 1920s and the 1950s the number of books banned in Ireland rose from a handful to thousands. To shrieks of "Eureka! I found a dirty word," the works of the likes of H.G. Wells, Orwell, Hemingway, and Chandler were declared off limits to Irish eyes. During this sad chapter, countless books by Irish writers—James Joyce, Frank O'Connor, Edna O'Brien, etc.—also had an unhappy ending. In a three-month period

in 1952, one member of the Censorship Board, C.J. O'Reilly, examined seventy books. He also banned seventy books! Ah, God be with the good oul' days.

BRehon laws: The Brehon Laws of ancient Ireland are now recognised as the most advanced legal system in the ancient world. Under Brehon Law, for example, women were equal partners in a marriage, of which there were ten forms. These included a marriage called the 7th degree union, which is extremely popular nowadays. It's called a one-night stand.

CELIBACY: If we've learned one thing about celibate priests in Ireland, it's that priests in Ireland largely aren't. And, in reality, there is no basis for them to be celibate in the first place. St. Peter was married and some popes were actually the daddies of other popes. Similarly, in ancient

Ireland, farmer traditionally begat farmer, judge begat judge, and priest begat priest. Until Pope Gregory VII came and screwed it up for everyone in 1079. After that, misery begat misery.

censorship:

Censorship in Ireland had reached such extremes in the 1930s through 1950s that the Church/State used to employ an army of folk to cut ads for lingerie out of foreign magazines coming into the country. During this sad era, thousands

of books, films, and even poems were banned or censored for containing the most innocuous references to sex or for using "swear words." So, to the bullies who would gladly return us to those dark days, we'd like to say the following: Arse. Boobs. Orgasm.

charles stewart parnell/kitty o'shea:

It was either the most famous or most infamous love story in Irish history, depending on your point of view. Parnell, MP and Irish Nationalist leader, had a fling with Kitty O'Shea, the missus

of a close party aide, William O'Shea. Surprisingly, Willie wasn't too put out, but when he decided to cut Kitty loose, the entire affair came out in the divorce proceedings. Parnell lost everything as a result. Except Kitty.

> In Ireland the inevitable never happens and the unexpected constantly occurs.
>
> —Sir John Pentland Mahaffy
> *Historian*
> *(1839–1919)*

churching: Up to the late 1960s, women who had given birth were expected to attend the ceremony of "churching," which involved them being blessed and "made pure again." (The service was unavailable to mothers of illegitimate kids.) It was, presumably, the act of conceiving the child that caused the woman to be impure in the first place, which, by extension, makes all of human existence a sin!

CLADDAGH RING: Perhaps because it's the handiest gadget ever invented to save girls the hassle of warding off unwanted attentions or encouraging wanted ones, the Claddagh Ring has attained global popularity. The ring features two hands holding a crowned heart, with the motto "let love and friendship reign." Association with Claddagh? No one has a clue.

RIGHT HAND

SINGLE
(I'M LOOKING FOR LOVE)

RIGHT HAND

HAVE BOYFRIEND
(I'M FALLING IN LOVE)

LEFT HAND

MARRIED
(I WISH I'D NEVER BOUGHT
THAT DAMN RING IN THE
FIRST PLACE)

On to practical matters. If you're a guy and want to check the availability of the talent/avoid a kick in the goolies, note the following: worn on the right hand, heart facing out, she's up for courtin'; right hand, heart facing in, there's a burly boyfriend about to clatter you for staring at his mot's hand; left hand, crown out, forget it—she's hitched.

clingfilm [plastic wrap]:

Necessity is the mother of invention, and incredible as it may seem to anyone under thirty, stories abound of the lengths some would go to in order to get around the State's ban on condoms up to 1985. The manufacturers advised us to "stretch the clingfilm tightly over the object, adhering it tightly to the sides and thus preventing any spillages." And that's exactly what a lot of people did . . .

IT'S SO USEFUL! COVERING CASSEROLES, KEEPING BREAD FRESH, HAVING A QUICK SHAG, WRAPPING PASTRIES...

coitus interruptus:

This was also a no-no, because "the spilling of the seed" interferes with "the natural consequences of sexual intercourse." However, this being Ireland, priests pulled out from denouncing it from the pulpit, as the details were too messy to go into. And, of course, their

relative silence on the subject was taken as tacit approval. During this period, sales of facial tissue went through the roof.

COMMITTEE ON EVIL LITERATURE: Not, as the name suggests, a group of righteous individuals doing battle with the forces of darkness, but the group which preceded the Censorship Board. Sitting for only one year, 1926, their recommendations set the standards for the strict censorship of the decades ahead. They are mentioned here only for their laughably dramatic title: for "Evil" read "Dirty."

FOR THE LAST TIME MAN YOU'VE GOT THE WRONG HOUSE! THE NAME'S JUST FOR DRAMATIC EFFECT.

COMMITTEE ON EVIL LITERATURE

condoms: These "Sheaths of Satan," as the religious right called them, were banned from 1935 to 1979, when Charlie Haughey came up with his famous "Irish solution to an Irish problem." Under that legislation, a doctor could prescribe condoms to those over eighteen, which was, ironically, two years older than the legal age for marriage!

What's more, the condoms had to be for "bona fide" family planning purposes, (i.e. couples couldn't get them if they just wanted a quick shag). The law was, of course, unenforceable, as the government couldn't insist on surveillance of love-making couples to keep an eye on their bona fides. It wasn't until 1985 that condoms became available without prescription.

confession: The back door through which we Irish Catholics could escape our guilt, especially about sex. As we fell helplessly into the jaws of passion, aware of the inevitability of mortal sin, we comforted ourselves with the thought that

> "I would not like to leave contraception on the long finger too long."
>
> —Jack Lynch
> *Taoiseach*
> *(1917–1999)*

tomorrow we would go to confession, say three Our Fathers and three Hail Marys and, Bob's yer uncle, we'd be grand with the Almighty again. So it seems God gave us guilt because he gave us sex, and confession because he gave us guilt. And in the divine plan, all three cancel each other out.

CONTRACEPTIVE BAN: It's amazing to think that up to 1935, contraceptives were actually available in Ireland. Then the government decided to outlaw their sale or import, a ban that would last until 1979. Not content with banjaxing the country's economy for decades, the government reminded people of their incompetence at literally every conceivable moment.

CONTRACEPTIVE TRAIN: On May 22, 1971, a group from the Irish Women's Liberation Movement put the campaign for access to contraception back on track. They took a train over the border into the heathen UK and bought

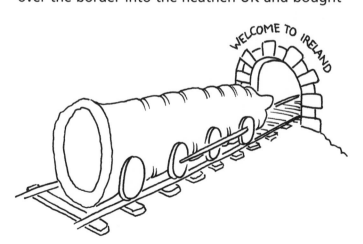

a gansey-load of contraceptives. Back in Dublin, they expected to be arrested for illegally importing the tools of the devil, but the authorities went limp under the media spotlight, and the women were allowed to pass. Thanks to the women on the "Durex Express," a major border had just been crossed.

COURTSHIP RITUALS: In olden days these involved such passion-killers as being chaperoned for weeks before being allowed out of parental sight and then making sure that there was "always room for the Holy Ghost" between you. Modern Irish courting rituals also severely restrict sexual activity, as they involve getting completely langered, jumping into bed, and then, before any funny business can happen, falling into an alcohol-induced coma.

YES HEIDI. THE 'SCATTERING' OF THE UNDERWEAR REALLY IS AN ANCIENT IRISH COURTSHIP RITUAL!

CROKE PARK: Believe it or not, the hallowed turf of Croker had its own small part to play in Irish sex/love lore, thanks to a story that hit the headlines in September 2002. Why? This was the first time someone scored at Croke Park Stadium while there was no game taking place. A courting couple, showing passion normally reserved for

> " I always had a reputation for going missing—Miss England, Miss United Kingdom, Miss World . . . "
>
> —George Best
> *Footballer*
> *(b.1946)*

the All Ireland Finals, scaled the gates after midnight, and by all accounts a lot of midfield action followed. It's not known how many shots they had, but they definitely had their own strip. The final result was that both midfielders were tackled by the Gardaí and sent off to court for a €500 fine. It will undoubtedly go down in GAA annals as a match that had a lot of physical contact.

dance halls: "Dens of Lust," "Agencies of Satan," "Vestibules of Hell"—these are some of the names given to dance halls by churchmen in the 1930s. In 1935 they persuaded the government to introduce the Public Dance Halls Act, which used the excuses of illicit drinking, safety concerns, etc. to close down hundreds of dance halls. In reality, the intention of the Act was to rid Ireland of an "immoral" influence and keep women firmly in their place—the kitchen.

ᴅιaʀᴍυιᴅ & ɢʀáιɴɴᴇ: Ireland's greatest mythological lovers. Gráinne, the High King's daughter, was to wed the aged Fionn McCool, but at the wedding feast she cast a spell on Fionn's pal, Diarmuid, who she fancied rotten. Diarmuid fled with her and they spent sixteen years legging it around Ireland. Eventually, after

a tussle with a magical boar, Diarmuid lies dying and only water carried by Fionn will save him, but Fionn lets the water slip through his fingers and Diarmuid croaks. Incidentally, you'll find "Diarmuid & Gráinne's beds" in forests or on

mountains all over Ireland, reputedly spots where they slept: evidence that Irish hotel prices were a rip-off even then.

Divorce: In early Celtic Ireland, grounds for divorce included sexual impotence due to gross obesity, telling tales about your love life, or being a thief. Then, in 1937, divorce was banned under the Constitution, so you couldn't legally dissolve your marriage on any grounds, including wife-beating, unfaithfulness, enduring decades of mental torture, etc. It's ironic that we can't say that the 1937 ban put us back in the Dark Ages, as in many ways the Dark Ages were much more enlightened.

ÐIVORCE REFERENÐA: In 1986, Ireland had its first divorce referendum. Six weeks before the poll, a huge majority wanted to remove the 1937 ban. Then the Catholic right mobilised! Divorce would lead to the end of the world, a plague of

> " Satire is a sort of glass, wherein beholders do generally discover everybody's face but their own. "
>
> —Oscar Wilde
> *Poet and Dramatist*
> *(1854–1900)*

locusts, and so on. Of course, the ban was upheld. We got another shot at it in 1995 and it was almost a rerun—a big lead for the "Yes" campaign almost reversed by sensationalist fear tactics. The ban was lifted, but only by a tiny majority. Jaysus, what were we like?

WELCOME TO
DUNGARVAN
TWINNED WITH
SODOM & GOMORRAH

ðungarvan: In 1995, Dungarvan (Pop. 5,700), was briefly the focus of international media attention when Father Michael Kennedy declared from the pulpit that a local woman had deliberately slept with over sixty locals to infect them with AIDS. Cue hundreds of suspicious glances from wives at husbands who were suddenly fascinated by the hymn sheet. The story spread like, well, a virus. Health experts, however, announced that the chances of a woman infecting so many men in this way were slim. Perversely, observers believe that this may have led to an increase in casual sex, which one assumes wasn't quite Father Kennedy's intention.

fallen women: Not girls who turned up in the Accident & Emergency ward with cuts on their knees, but those who committed the greatest of all sins—getting preggers. The problem is that it's so bleedin' visible. A pregnant single girl wandering around the village for nine months, reminding everyone that they had wobbly bits, was unthinkable. The solution was for her family to pack her off to a home so everyone could stop thinking about their thingies and return to singing songs about the Famine.

fallen men: As yet, historians have not found any records of this species, so it is assumed that all the fallen women were impregnated by some form of mysterious airborne sperm.

father michael cleary: In the mid-1990s it emerged that another well-known cleric, Michael Cleary, had fathered a child. Known as "the singing priest," Father Cleary was out of tune with his own preaching on the evils of extra-marital sex and on priestly celibacy. It didn't really bother most people that he'd had a child, just that he'd had the nerve to make such a song and dance about his flock's sexual activities!

...AND THIS WEEK, INSTEAD OF A SERMON I'm GOING TO SING "IF I SAID YOU HAD A BEAUTIFUL BODY WOULD YOU HOLD IT AGAINST ME..."

[GIVING BIRTH TO A] FOOTBALL TEAM:

Nowadays, family size in Ireland conforms pretty much to the norm, i.e. 2.7465 kids. But at one point, the average number of kids in an Irish family was ten! There are many explanations for these ultra-large families—no contraception,

> " *Children begin by loving their parents; after a time they judge them; rarely, if ever, do they forgive them.* "
>
> —Oscar Wilde
> *Poet and Dramatist*
> *(1854–1900)*

preference for male children, young marriage age. The real reason is that Irish men and women are clearly the most fertile and sexually adept people on the planet.

GAY IRELAND:

Up to the 1970s, the only "Gay" living in Ireland presented *The Late Late Show*. For most Irish people, through ignorance, innocence, or denial, homosexuality did not exist.

But the wider world was opening up to us in the form of travel, films, multi-channel TV, literature, etc. And before we knew it, everyone had come out of the closet, in terms of awareness at least, of the gay community's existence. Homosexual acts were decriminalised in 1993, and as a measure of how far we've come since then, we've had a couple of gay lads snogging on our most popular early evening soap. Ireland's first gay/lesbian Taoiseach can't be far behind.

GIRLIE MAGAZINES: Up to 1996, the long-suffering men of Ireland had to go to great lengths to enjoy the beauties cavorting naked in *Playboy* magazine, as girlie mags were banned.

To keep abreast of the latest centrefolds, you had to smuggle one in from some exotic place (like Newry or Birmingham) and risk being stigmatised for years. Nowadays you can get loads of mags with naked ladies. Or, for *Mná na hÉireann*, naked men. Did ye ever think we'd see the day?

> Niagara Falls is the bride's second great disappointment.
>
> —Oscar Wilde
> *Poet and Dramatist*
> *(1854–1900)*

handfasting: Part of the ancient marriage ritual in which the couple getting married were literally hitched to each other with a rope around the wrists. In those enlightened days the trial marriage lasted 366 days. Then, if the wife discovered that the hubby was, say, an alco with a sheep fetish, or he learned that his missus only changed her knickers once a year, they could tell

each other to shag off when the period was up. This is where the term "tying the knot" originated. In some versions of the ritual, the knots couldn't be untied until the marriage had been consummated. Kinky, those Celts, eh?

MA, THIS IS MY GIRLFRIEND BOOBSY. I MET HER THROUGH A SMALL AD IN 'IN DUBLIN.'

In ∂ublIn magazIne: From its launch in the 1970s, Dubliners knew that the easiest place to find sex was between the pages of this event guide. Not that it featured overt porn, but almost as titillating were the ads for massage parlours (brothels), the small ads for dirty videos, and of course, its personal ads, some genuine, some not so. A typical one might run: "Girl, 20s, large assets, seeks man for social intercourse. Bring money." Who knows, maybe she really did just

want to have a chat and the money was to feed the gas meter?

Internet: A brief search using the words "Ireland" and "sex" reveals that inhibition has become a dirty word. Any sexual liaison can be arranged—man/woman, man/man, woman/woman, couple/woman—you name it. Want sex toys, edible lingerie, or a vibrating bed with mirrored ceiling? No problem. And apparently a big hit with Irish couples are silk bands for tying up one's partner. Must be something to do with our 700 years of bondage.

Irish family planning association: Without the IFPA's tireless fight for contraceptive rights, it's probably safe to say that our largely

THE IFPA DON'T BELIEVE IN THE SANCTITY OF LIFE. YEAH. LET'S BLOW THEM UP.

impotent political masters would still be wondering if a spermicidal jelly would be nice with custard.

kissing: Mothers and priests didn't discourage the widespread belief among young Irish girls that you could get pregnant through French kissing. Possibly where the word "misconception" came from.

> Lord! I wonder what fool it was that first invented kissing.
>
> —Jonathan Swift
> *Author and Dean of St. Patrick's Cathedral*
> *(1667–1745)*

knock marriage bureau: Set up in 1969 and run by a local priest, the bureau has been responsible for arranging almost 900 marriages. And, at just €80 a pop, you could end up with a marriage licence for less than a TV licence.

> When the blind lead the blind,
> no wonder they both fall into—
> matrimony.
>
> —George Farquhar
> *Poet and Dramatist*
> *(1678–1707)*

laд lane: The most appropriately named lane in Ireland, if not in the world. Lad, in case you're unaware, is a Dublin slang word for, eh, willy. And Lad Lane is the place where you're most likely to see one in action, as it is frequented by ladies of the night. It's probably just a coincidence, but it's nice to think that Dublin's "working girls" chose Lad Lane as a place of business because they've got a really good sense of humour.

lap дanciнg clubs: First appeared in Dublin in the mid-1990s and have since spread to every corner of the country. Most of the performers are English girls or from Eastern Europe; Irish girls

are still probably worried they'll end up dancing for their Da. In 2002, the shocked residents of the Kildare village of Milltown discovered that they had a lap dancing club in their tiny backwater. Surely not what de Valera envisioned—comely maidens lapdancing at the crossroads?

> Girls like to be played with,
> and rumpled a little too, sometimes.
>
> —Oliver Goldsmith
> *Poet and Writer*
> *(1728–1774)*

[the] late late show: The Catholic, right-wing politician Oliver J. Flanagan once remarked that there was no sex in Ireland before TV. More accurately, there was no sex before *The Late Late Show*. Its host, Gay Byrne, shocked us unworldly Paddies by shooting the breeze with lesbian nuns or demonstrating the use of a condom with his finger. In an earlier show, Gay had a mock version of the Mr. & Mrs. quiz in which he asked a

contestant what she wore in bed on her honeymoon night. Her joking reply of "nothing" brought a torrent of condemnation. How innocent we were . . .

Lent: In the old days, you were encouraged to abstain from many things during Lent: meat, drinking, sweets, dancing, getting married, carnal pleasures, swearing, and general merrymaking. That left knitting.

lisdoonvarna matchmaking festival:

Lisdoonvarna in County Clare was originally famed for the healing power of its natural spa. Nowadays, Lisdoonvarna invites you to dip your toe in the waters of romance, or any other bodily part if you get lucky. Every September thousands flock there, hoping to meet the woman/man of their dreams, as a couple of local horse-traders (literally) carry on a 200-year-old tradition of matching lonely hearts. The various stallions/fillies chew the cud over vast quantities of booze and negotiate the hurdles of getting to know one another. And if the girl gets really lucky, she'll discover she's found a stud.

SOMETHING TELLS ME OUR MATCHMAKERS ARE LOSING THEIR TOUCH...

LISTEN FATHER, I SAW FIONA BENDING OVER THE FREEZER AND I HAD LUSTFUL THOUGHTS- I COULDN'T HELP IT. I HAD TO MAKE LOVE TO HER THERE AND THEN. SO FATHER, WILL I BE BANNED FROM THE CHURCH?

BANNED? OF COURSE NOT! WHY WOULD YOU BE BANNED?

CAUSE THEY BANNED US FROM THE SUPERMARKET.

lustful thoughts: One of the Church's biggest hobby horses during Ireland's Dark Ages (1930s–1990s) was the sin of lustful thoughts. Records show that monks whose thoughts strayed inside another's underwear were rewarded with a year on bread and water. Of course, policing this relied purely on one's honesty. Imagine a woman confessing lustful thoughts to the local priest, who then has lustful thoughts about her lustful thoughts. He confesses to the canon, giving him lustful notions. He must then confess to

the bishop . . . the archbishop . . . the cardinal. Eventually, someone has to keep schtum and be damned! Doesn't bear thinking about.

MARRIAGE: In Brehon times there were up to ten forms of marriage. In twentieth century Ireland, marriage had only one form—insoluble. So you had better not make a pig's arse of

> For our wedding we both agreed to a small affair.
> So I had a fling with a waiter.
> —Sinead Murphy
> *Irish Writer*
> *(b.1959)*

picking your mate, because whatever happened you'd be stuck with him/her for eternity. The other thing about Irish marriage was that it was the only way to legitimately get laid. This was called the 15,000-night stand.

massage parlours: In the 1980s/1990s anyone in search of a genuine massage was likely to find parts of his anatomy tended to that wouldn't be found in a physiotherapist's handbook. Ads featuring "Massage Parlour" usually meant "Brothel." But common as this knowledge was, numerous Garda raids indicated that countless politicians, clergy, and lawyers made this mistake and went seeking treatment for a particular muscle which had gone into spasm.

masturbation: Bodily self-abuse, self-defilement, or self-pollution, as it used to be called, besides being a mortal sin, produced a range of side-effects that were God's way of punishing us. Among these were blindness, stunted growth, gradual insanity, growth of hair on palms, acne. At least that's what our short, spotty, hairy, specky lune of a teacher told us.

monto: "The Monto" was Dublin's thriving red light district from 1870 until 1925. At one time, up to 1,200 ladies offered their wares in the Montgomery Street (now Foley Street) area, making it Europe's largest red light district. The Monto was frequented by many notables, including King Edward VII, presumably so he could personally acquaint his subjects with the royal sceptre.

most lustful man in Ireland: This title perhaps goes to the last High King of Ireland, Ruaidhrí Ó Conchobhair, (died in 1198, probably

from exhaustion). Old Ruaidhrí is reputed to have had his wicked way with so many women that it became too much for the Pope, who had to satisfy himself with a handful. He offered to forgive Ruaidhrí if he would confine himself to having sex with just six women. Ruaidhrí's reply? "You mean, at the same time?"

MOVIE BANS: There have been thousands over the last century, including *Brief Encounter* (1946) for an extra-marital affair, *Ulysses* (1967) for obscene language, *The Life of Brian* (1979) for blasphemy, *From Dusk 'till Dawn* (1996) for

violence. But for every three banned, ten "dirty" movies were allowed through—after they'd been slashed to ribbons. See, with movies, it's easy to snip out people's naughty bits. This resulted in scenes like:

Jane: Frank! I want you to make me feel like a wom—

Frank: I better get to work, it's almost nine.

Jane: You sure you won't join me in the shower?

Frank: Yes, waiter, I'll have the steak.

[the] pill: Incredibly, given the era's anti-contraception frenzy, the Pill was available here in 1963. Had they suddenly decided to allow us let our hair down, not to mention our undies?

SHE SAYS SHE'S TAKING THE
THE PILL AS A CYCLE REGULATOR.

YEAH SURE. AND I SUPPOSE THAT'S
WHY THEY CALL HER 'THE BICYCLE!'

'Course not! Doctors could prescribe the Pill only as a cycle regulator. And good Catholic women using it thus would never stoop to taking advantage of its other side-effect: consequence-free sex. Unfortunately, if your doctor wouldn't prescribe the Pill, the only other legal oral contraceptive available was the word "No."

polygamy: In pre-Christian Ireland, it was accepted practice for men (particularly wealthy ones) to have several wives, and though the Church opposed this when they arrived, polygamy endured for centuries. The official reason for having lots of wives was to have lots of male heirs. The unofficial reason was so that rich men could have an unlimited supply of sex.

> Bigamy is having one wife too many. Monogamy is the same.
>
> —Oscar Wilde
> *Poet and Dramatist*
> *(1854–1900)*

The result was that these guys often had over thirty kids. Imagine what it was like trying to get a turn in the bathroom in the morning!

PREGNANCY: When occurring out of wedlock, it was traditional to describe the pregnant lass by one of the following quaint old Irish phrases: "Up the pole," "Up the flue," "In the family way," "A bun in the oven," "About to drop a chisler."

> "The midwife said that the agony of having a child could last a long time. I didn't realise she meant eighteen years."
> —Sinead Murphy
> *Irish Writer*
> *(b.1959)*

For the correct usage of these expressions, please note that they were traditionally muttered under the breath.

queen maeve: A definite contender for Ireland's most lustful woman, Maeve supposedly lived around the first century B.C. and her most famous adventure is recorded in *The Táin* (*The Cattle Raid of Cooley*). But it was her sexual adventures that were really legendary. As a sort of staff incentive scheme, Maeve would offer her "willing thighs" to her bravest warriors and was reputed to have had as many as thirty men a day! And to think, this sex-machine's face used to grace our £1 note . . .

rhythm method: The only form of family planning officially endorsed by Church and State up to almost the end of the last century. But

because they were too embarrassed to fully explain the technique to anyone, based as it was on the woman's menstrual cycle, lots of girls decided to interpret the title as meaning it was safe to have sex immediately after a bit of fervent dancing to the local showband.

school dances: For many an Irish youth, this was the first contact he/she would have with the opposite sex. Actually, contact is too strong a

> Dancing: the vertical expression
> of a horizontal desire.
> —George Bernard Shaw
> *Dramatist*
> *(1856–1950)*

word, as any boob/chest interaction would earn you a poke of a stick in the ear from the supervising brother/nun. Nuns reputedly wouldn't let girls wear shiny shoes in case boys

could see a reflection of their knickers. Only dancing and talking was allowed. The talking inevitably got around to getting the hell out of there and finding somewhere to have a grope.

SEX: In Ireland this was an eight-letter word spelled m-a-r-r-i-a-g-e. Premarital sex was not so much frowned upon as trodden upon. But there was a possible escape clause. If you were chastised

> While I was a teenager I wasn't allowed any sexual freedom. So I had to settle for bondage.
>
> —Sinead Murphy
> *Irish Writer*
> *(b.1959)*

for considering premarital sex, you could always inform the priest that it wasn't premarital if you never intended to get married.

sex education: In Ireland, sex education was traditionally provided by religious orders for whom sex did not officially exist—so no need for sex education. Parents stuck to "the stork

brought you" story, so sex education was confined to sniggered whispers behind the school shed. Here you had your first lesson in the anatomy of the opposite sex, the geometry of which bit went where and the mathematical impossibility of this ever happening to you. It was also where every thirteen-year-old first learned that intercourse wasn't the exam you sat in third year.

sheela-na-gigs: Ancient stone carvings of women blatantly displaying their naughty bits. The carvings predate Christianity and were possibly part of early fertility rites and a celebration of female sexuality. The gas thing is that the place you're most likely to find one of these shameless hussies is above the doorway of a church!

(the) spike: Not the yoke on O'Connell Street, but a short-lived RTÉ TV series in the late 1970s that was as hotly debated as the Keane/McCarthy

affair. The fifth episode featured a woman posing nude for an art class. Of course, the entire country tuned in to watch. Condemnation (and axing of the series) swiftly followed, and, most famously, the founder of the League of Decency suffered a heart attack after watching the scene. Imagine how they'd have reacted to *Sex and the City*?

st. valentine: The patron saint of mushy greeting cards—sorry—love, whose remains are reputed to lie in Dublin's Whitefriar Street Church, a gift from Pope Gregory XVI in 1835. Before he was martyred in Rome on February 14, AD 269, he miraculously cured his jailor's blind

daughter and sent her a message signed "from your Valentine." But that's probably a load of crap. He's now a global industry, his name adorning cards, inflatable hearts, even sex toys! The inscription on his casket reads: Roses are red, violets are blue . . . (only kidding).

terms of endearment:

Expressions of endearment in Gaeilge can be found in Irish literature stretching back millennia. Among the most popular to survive are: *A ghrá mo chroí* (Love of my heart), *Mo mhúirnín bán* (My beautiful darling), and *Póg mo thóin* (Kiss my arse). That last one has the benefit that it can be used both as an expression of anger and of affection.

WELL SHE SAID 'BA MHAITH LIOM CUPLA FOCAL' AND I SAID ' I WOULDN'T MIND A SHAG MYSELF!..

unfortunate girls: The term given to prostitutes in the early part of the last century. In those days many girls arrived in the capital from impoverished rural homes in search of work, often to be abused by their employers, and then turned to prostitution in desperation. Today, of course, that's all changed. Now the girls come from impoverished countries in Eastern Europe to be abused by their employers.

> There is no magician like Love.
> —Marguerite Blessington
> *Countess of Blessington*
> *(1789–1849)*

VIAGRA: Given Ireland's sexual history, it's paradoxical that the small town of Ringaskiddy in Cork should be the place that, since the mid-1990s, has been giving a lift to people's sex lives all over the world. Since U.S. drug giant Pfizer

> "Modesty is a quality in a lover more praised by the women than liked."
>
> —Richard Brinsley Sheridan
> *Playwright*
> *(1751–1816)*

erected their Viagra plant, the area's previously limp economy has grown enormously and earned it the nickname Viagra Falls. The local name for the drug is "De Pfizer Riser," and rumours have abounded of a baby boom in the area due to emissions from the plant, but the hard facts refute this. Aside from that, it seems that unless sex suddenly becomes unpopular, the town's fortunes will continue to rise and rise.

VIRGINITY: One of the traditional Irish ways to scare girls into retaining their virginity was for a nun to pull the petals off a flower, then ask one of the class to come up and replace them.

Impossible, of course, and it was equally impossible to get your virginity back. And what man would want a flower with no petals? This practice gave the English language the term "to deflower." It also gave us a huge number of really pissed-off gardeners.

three

massive songs

yer oul' fella always
sang when he was
jarred at a hooley

feel free
to sing along

If there's one thing the Irish are famed the world over for, it's their willingness to spontaneously break into song. Yet somehow, they remain in blissful ignorance of the fact that they're singing voice sounds like a sack of cats thrown onto a bonfire.

See, if you're Irish, your vocal skills are far less important than your readiness to sing along with great enthusiasm to the likes of "Danny Boy," "Whiskey in the Jar," or "The Waxies' Dargle."

Here, in all their glory, are every word, every line, and every chorus of the most popular Irish songs ever written. Which means you'll always be able to join in with your few bars, no matter how many bars you've been to!

the Banks of my own lovely lee

John Fitzgerald

The Cork National Anthem, as it is also known, is just one in a long line of ballads in which an exile laments the loss of his homeland. There he is in America, loaded with spondulicks, dreaming of all he's left behind: freezing cold, no plumbing, no food. And he wants to come back? Were they all feckin' nuts?

How oft do my thoughts in their fancy take flight
To the home of my childhood away,
To the days when each patriot's vision seemed bright
Ere I dreamed that those joys should decay.
When my heart was as light as the wild winds that blow
Down the Mardyke through each elm tree,
Where I sported and played 'neath each green leafy shade
On the banks of my own lovely Lee.
Where I sported and played...

And then in the springtime of laughter and song
Can I ever forget the sweet hours?
With the friends of my youth as we rambled along
'Mongst the green mossy banks and wild flowers.
Then when the evening sun sinking to rest
Sheds its golden light over the sea

The maid with her lover the wild daisies pressed
On the banks of my own lovely Lee.
The maid with her lover...

'Tis a beautiful land this dear isle of song
Its gems shed their light to the world
And her faithful sons bore thro' ages of wrong,
The standard St. Patrick unfurled.
Oh would I were there with the friends I love best
And my fond bosom's partner with me,
We'd roam thy banks over, and when weary we'd rest
By thy waters, my own lovely Lee.
We'd roam thy banks over...

Oh what joys should be mine ere this life should decline
To seek shells on thy sea-girdled shore.
While the steel-feathered eagle, oft splashing the brine
Brings longing for freedom once more.
Oh all that on earth I wish for or crave
Is that my last crimson drop be for thee,
To moisten the grass of my forefathers' grave
On the banks of my own lovely Lee.
To moisten the grass of...

the black velvet band

Traditional

A cautionary tale for you young bucks that get all gooey-eyed at the sight of a pretty face and a fine pair of hips. Beware! She's the devil in disguise, bent on leading you astray and whisking you off to Van Dieman's Land for seven years. Or nowadays to the Costa del Sol for fourteen days, which, when you think of it, is probably worse.

In a neat little town they call Belfast,
Apprenticed to trade I was bound,
And many's the hour of sweet happiness,
I spent in that neat little town,
Till a strange misfortune overtook me,
Which caused me to stray from the land,
Far away from my friends and relations,
Betrayed by the black velvet band.

Chorus:
Her eyes they shone like diamonds,
You'd think her the queen of the land,
And her hair hung over her shoulder,
Tied up with a black velvet band.

As I went walking down Broadway,
Not intending to stay very long,
Who should I see but a fine colleen,
As she came a-traipsing along.

A watch she pulled out of her pocket,
And slipped it right into my hand,
On the very first day that I met her,
Bad luck to the black velvet band.

Chorus

Before the judge and the jury,
Next morning we both did appear,
And the gentleman swore to the jury,
The case was proven quite clear.
For seven years transportation,
Down to the Van Dieman's Land,
Far away from my friends and relations,
To follow her black velvet band.

I SENTENCE YOU
TO TWO WEEKS
IN LANZAROTE

Chorus

Oh all you brave young fellows,
A warning now take you from me,
Beware of the pretty young damsels,
You might meet around in Tralee.
They'll treat you to whiskey and porter,
Until you're unable to stand,
And before you have time for to leave them,
You'll be sent down to Van Dieman's Land.

Bunch of thyme

Traditional

This might seem an odd one, but thyme in this instance appears to be a metaphor for virginity. Or one could say that in more innocent days it was a metaphor for innocence. Then again, it could be a metaphor for youth. Or for time. Or maybe the whole thing is just a recipe for vegetable bleedin' soup.

Come all ye maidens young and fair,
All you that are blooming in your prime.
Always beware and keep your garden fair,
Let no man steal away your thyme.

Chorus:
For thyme it is a precious thing,
And thyme brings all things to my mind.
Thyme with all its flavours, along with all its joys,
Thyme brings all things to my mind.

Once I had a bunch of thyme,
I thought it never would decay.
Then came a lusty sailor, who chanced to pass my way,
and stole my bunch of thyme away.

Chorus

The sailor gave to me a rose,
A rose that never would decay.
He gave it to me to keep me reminded
Of when he stole my thyme away.

Chorus

VERY TASTY. I WOULDN'T MIND SOME OF THAT!!!

"[Ireland is]. . . a land of cosy homesteads. . . with comely maidens dancing at the crossroads."

—Éamon de Valera
Irish President and Taoiseach
(1882–1975)

the cliffs of dooneen

Traditional

This one is a big favourite at sing-songs, thanks mainly to the fact that a well-known Irish folk band popularised it in the seventies. However, most drunken party-goers usually only get about as far as "Watching all the wild flowers la da da di da..." or thereabouts. They then quickly descend into "Na na lan di da. Da di da na di da da la...the cliffs of Dooneen."

You may travel far far from your own native home,
Far away o'er the mountains, far away o'er the foam,
But of all the fine places that I've ever been
Sure there's none can compare with the cliffs of Dooneen.

Take a view o'er the mountains, fine sights you'll see there,
You'll see the high rocky mountains o'er the west coast of Clare;
Oh the towns of Kilkee and Kilrush can be seen
From the high rocky slopes round the cliffs of Dooneen.

AH THE CLIFFS OF DOO...HIC...NEEN...

It's a nice place to be on a fine summer's day
Watching all the wild flowers that ne'er do decay,
Oh the hares and lofty pheasants are plain to be seen,
Making homes for their young round the cliffs of Dooneen.

Fare thee well to Dooneen, fare thee well for a while,
And to all the kind people I'm leaving behind;
To the streams and the meadows where late I have been
And the high rocky slopes round the cliffs of Dooneen.

> "Ireland is where strange tales begin and happy endings are possible."
>
> —Charles Haughey
> *Taoiseach*
> *(b.1925)*

danny boy

Fred Weatherly

When me Auntie Maureen used to sing this—Ireland's favourite song of love and death—it never failed to bring a tear to me eye. I swear, her voice really was that bad.

Oh Danny boy, the pipes, the pipes are calling,
From glen to glen, and down the mountain side.
The summer's gone, and all the flowers are dying,
'Tis you, 'tis you must go and I must bide.

But come you back when summer's in the meadow,
Or when the valley's hushed and white with snow,
'Tis I'll be here in sunshine or in shadow,
Oh Danny boy, oh Danny boy, I love you so.

SOMEONE SHUT HER UP. I CAN'T
TAKE MUCH MORE OF THIS!

And if you come, when all the flowers are dying,
And I am dead, as dead I well may be,
You'll come and find the place where I am lying,
And kneel and say an "Ave" there for me.

And I shall hear, though soft you tread above me,
And all my dreams will warmer, sweeter be.
And you will kneel and tell me that you love me,
And I shall sleep in peace until you come to me.

"There is no language like the Irish
for soothing and quieting."
—John Millington Synge
Poet and Dramatist
(1871–1909)

Galway Bay

Francis A. Fahey

In the final verse, the singer exhorts God to grant him his personal heaven by returning him home to his beloved Galway. Fair enough. But if such a system is actually in operation, I wonder, God, could I have Bermuda?

It's far away I am today
From scenes I roamed a boy,
And long ago the hour, I know
I first saw Illinois.
But time nor tide, not waters wide,
Can wean my heart away,
For ever true it flies to you
My own dear Galway Bay.

A prouder man I'd walk the land
In health and peace of mind,
If I might toil and strive and moil,
Nor cast one thought behind;
But what would be the world to me,
Its rank and rich array,
If memory I lost of thee,
My poor old Galway Bay.

Oh, grey and bleak, by shore and creek,
The rugged rocks abound,
But sweeter green the grass between

Than grows on Irish ground.
So friendship fond, all wealth beyond,
And love that lives always,
Bless each poor home beside your foam,
My dear old Galway Bay.

Had I youth's blood and hopeful mood
And heart of fire once more,
For all the gold the earth might hold,
I'd never quit your shore;
I'd live content whate'er God sent,
With neighbours old and grey,
And lay my bones 'neath churchyard stone
Beside you, Galway Bay.

The blessing of a poor old man
Be with you night and day,
The blessings of a lonely man
Whose heart will soon be clay.
'Tis all the Heaven I'd ask of God
Upon my dying day,
My soul to soar forevermore
Above you, Galway Bay.

the holy ground

Traditional

The basic story is this: Man leaves girl to go to sea, promising to return. Storm hits ship. Ship survives. Man goes to pub, gets locked. Man returns to sea. Forgets about girl. Typical Irish male.

Fare thee well, my lovely Dinah, a thousand times adieu.
We are bound away from the Holy Ground and
    the girls we love so true.
We'll sail the salt seas over and we'll return for sure,
To see again the girls we love and the Holy
    Ground once more.

I LOVE YOU.

Chorus:
(Yelled) Fine girl you are!
(Sung) You're the girl that I adore,
And still I live in hope to see the Holy Ground once more.
(Yelled) Fine girl you are!

Now when we're out a-sailing and you are far behind,
Fine letters will I write to you with the secrets of my mind.
The secrets of my mind, my girl, you're the girl that I adore,
And still I live in hope to see the Holy Ground once more.

Chorus

Oh now the storm is raging and we are far from shore,
The poor old ship she's sinking fast and the rigging is all tore.
The night is dark and dreary, we can scarcely see the moon,
But still I live in hope to see the Holy Ground once more.

Chorus

And now the storm is over and we are safe on shore,
We'll drink a toast to the Holy Ground and the girls
   that we adore.
We'll drink strong ale and porter and we'll make
   the rafters roar,
And when our money is all spent we'll go to sea once more.

Chorus

> A man travels the world over
> in search of what he needs and
> returns home to find it.
>
> —George Moore
> *Writer*
> *(1852–1933)*

i'll take you home again, kathleen

Thomas Westendorf

Ah, what a great old traditional Irish song! Except that it's not Irish at all. It was written by a German called Westendorf while he was living in Illinois. Kathleen, his missus, was always whingeing about going back to the old sod (Ireland that is, not Westendorf), so he wrote this for her, to shut her up.

I'll take you home again, Kathleen,
Across the ocean wild and wide.
To where your heart has ever been,
Since first you were my bonnie bride.
The roses all have left your cheek,
I've watched them fade away and die;
Your voice is sad when e'er you speak
And tears bedim your loving eyes.

Chorus:
Oh, I will take you back, Kathleen,
To where your heart will feel no pain,
And when the fields are fresh and green
I'll take you to your home again.

I know you love me, Kathleen, dear,
Your heart was ever fond and true.
I always feel when you are near
That life holds nothing dear but you.
The smiles that once you gave to me
I scarcely ever see them now,
Though many, many times I see
A dark'ning shadow on your brow.

Chorus

To that dear home beyond the sea,
My Kathleen shall again return.
And when thy old friends welcome thee,
Thy loving heart will cease to yearn.
Where laughs the little silver stream,
Beside your mother's humble cot,
And brightest rays of sunshine gleam,
There all your grief will be forgot.

Chorus

WOULD YOU C'MON
KATHLEEN, IT'S WAY
PAST CLOSING TIME!

I'll tell me ma

Traditional

Next time you're singing away happily to this one, take pause for a moment during the song to ask yourself one simple question: "How the hell can anyone wear bells on their toes?" Must be a Belfast thing.

I'll tell me ma, when I go home,
The boys won't leave the girls alone,
They pulled my hair and stole my comb,
And that's alright till I go home.

Chorus:
She is handsome, she is pretty,
She is the belle of Belfast city.
She is courtin', one, two, three.
Please, won't you tell me who is she?

Albert Mooney says he loves her,
All the boys are fighting for her.
They rap at the door and ring at the bell,
Saying "Oh my true love, are you well?"
Out she comes as white as snow,
Rings on her fingers, bells on her toes,
Old Johnny Murray says she'll die,
If she doesn't get the fellow with the roving eye.

Chorus

Let the wind and the rain and the hail blow high,
And the snow come tumblin' from the sky,
She's as sweet as apple pie,
And she'll get her own lad by and by.
When she gets a lad of her own,
She won't tell her ma when she comes home,
Let them all come as they will,
But it's Albert Mooney she loves still.

Chorus

GET YOUR TOE BELLS, TWO FOR A POUND. TOE BELLS TWO FOR A POUND!!!

the IRISH ROVER

Traditional

This is one of those tunes that when your Da or your uncle starts crowing it at the hooley after the wedding, it seems to last forever, or at least as long as it took the Irish Rover to wander the high seas. And all the while you're left standing there, stupid false grin on your gob, pretending to tap your foot to the tune and dying to go to the bar for a pint. So remember, as soon as it stops, it's time to abandon ship.

In the year of our Lord, eighteen hundred and six
We set sail from the fair cove of Cork.
We were bound far away with a cargo of bricks
For the fine city hall of New York.
In a very fine craft, she was rigged fore and aft
And oh, how the wild winds drove her.
She had twenty-three masts and withstood many a blast
And we called her the Irish Rover.

There was Barney McGee from the banks of the Lee,
There was Hogan from County Tyrone.
There was Johnny McGurk who was scared stiff of work
And a chap from Westmeath called Malone.
There was Slugger O'Toole who was drunk as a rule,
And fighting Bill Casey from Dover.
There was Dooley from Clare who was strong as a bear,
And was skipper of the Irish Rover.

We had one million bales of old billy goats' tails,
We had two million buckets of stones.
We had three million sides of old blind horses hides,
We had four million packets of bones.
We had five million hogs, we had six million dogs,
And seven million barrels of porter.
We had eight million bags of the best Sligo rags
In the hold of the Irish Rover.

We had sailed seven years when the measles broke out
And the ship lost her way in a fog.
And the whole of the crew was reduced unto two,
'Twas myself and the captain's old dog.
Then the ship struck a rock. Oh Lord, what a shock,
And then she heeled right over,
Turned nine times around, and the poor dog was drowned,
I'm the last of the Irish Rover.

lanigan's ball

Neil Bryant/Tony Pastor

Besides the usual content of death, war, tragedy, butchered innocents, famine, etc., occasionally we Irish find room for a laugh in our musical hearts. But don't get too used to it, we'll be back to the blood and the broken hearts before you know it. In fact, normal service will resume just as soon as Lanigan has held his rather lengthy ball.

In the town of Athy one Jeremy Lanigan,
Battered away 'til he hadn't a pound.
His father he died and made him a man again,
Left him a farm and ten acres of ground.
He gave a grand party to friends and relations
Who didn't forget him when sent to the wall,
And if you'll but listen I'll make your eyes glisten
Of the rows and the ructions of Lanigan's Ball.

Chorus:
Six long months I spent in Dublin,
Six long months doing nothing at all.
Six long months I spent in Dublin,
Learning to dance for Lanigan's Ball.

Myself to be sure got free invitations,
For all the nice girls and boys I might ask,
And just in a minute both friends and relations
Were dancing as merry as bees 'round a cask.

Judy O'Daly, that nice little milliner,
She tipped me a wink for to give her a call,
And I soon arrived with Timothy Galligan
Just in good time for Lanigan's Ball.

Chorus

There were lashings of punch and wine for the ladies,
Potatoes and cakes; there was bacon and tea.
There were the Nolans, Dolans, O'Gradys
Courting the girls and dancing away.
Songs they went 'round as plenty as water,
"The harp that once sounded in Tara's old hall,"
"Sweet Nelly Gray" and "The Rat Catcher's Daughter,"
All singing together at Lanigan's Ball.

Chorus

They were doing all kinds of nonsensical polkas
All 'round the room in a great whirly-gig.
Julia and I, we banished their nonsense
And tipped them the twist of a reel and a jig.

And oh how the girls they got all mad at me
Danced 'til you'd think the ceiling would fall.
For I spent three weeks at Brooks' Academy
Learning new steps for Lanigan's Ball.

Chorus

Boys were all merry and the girls they were hearty,
And danced all around in couples and groups.
'Til an accident happened, young Terence McCarthy,
He put his right leg through Miss Finnerty's hoops.
The poor creature fainted and cried, "Meelia murther,"
Called for her brothers and gathered them all.
Carmody swore that he'd go no further
'Til he'd had satisfaction at Lanigan's Ball.

Chorus

In the midst of the row Miss Kerrigan fainted,
Her cheeks at the same time as red as a rose.
Some of the lads declared she was painted,
She took a small drop too much, I suppose.

Her sweetheart, Ned Morgan, so powerful and able,
When he saw his fair colleen stretched out by the wall,
He tore the left leg from under the table
And smashed all the dishes at Lanigan's Ball.

Chorus

Boys, oh boys, 'twas then there were runctions.
Myself got a lick from big Phelim McHugh.
But I soon replied to his kind introduction
And kicked up a terrible hullabaloo.
Old Casey, the piper, was near being strangled,
They squeezed up his pipes, bellows, chanters and all.
The girls in their ribbons, they got all entangled,
And that put an end to Lanigan's Ball.

> "Ah, we men and women
> are like ropes drawn tight
> with strain that pull us
> different ways."
> —Bram Stoker
> *Novelist*
> *(1847–1912)*

leaving of liverpool

Traditional

Okay, strictly speaking this isn't Irish. Come to think of it, loosely speaking it isn't Irish either. But it does crop up regularly at Irish sing-songs and it does have all the basic ingredients. It's akin to one of those Brits we've adopted as one of our own—like St. Patrick. And we'll allow it the great privilege of being Irish for as long as we can get something out of it for nothing.

Farewell to Prince's Landing Stage,
River Mersey, fare thee well.
I am bound for California,
A place I know right well.

Chorus:
So fare thee well, my own true love,
When I return united we will be.
It's not the leaving of Liverpool that's grieving me
But my darling when I think of thee.

I'm bound off for California
By the way of stormy Cape Horn.
And I'm bound to write you a letter, love,
When I am homeward bound.

Chorus

I have signed on a Yankee Clipper ship,
Davy Crockett is her name.
And Burgess is the captain of her,
And they say she's a floating hell.

Chorus

I have shipped with Burgess once before,
And I think I know him well.
If a man's a seaman, he can get along,
If not, then he's sure in hell.

Chorus

LIVERPOOL 0:
WYCOMBE 3
THAT'S IT.
I'M LEAVING.

Farewell to lower Frederick Street,
Ensign Terrace and Park Lane.
For I think it will be a long, long time
Before I see you again.

Chorus

Oh the sun is on the harbour, love,
And I wish I could remain,
For I know it will be a long, long time
Before I see you again.

maids when you're young never wed an old man

Traditional

The filthiest, most suggestive, rudest, and most downright offensive song you're ever likely to hear sung at an Irish social function. Now, bet you're dying to read the lyrics!

An old man came courting me, hey ding doorum-da,
An old man came courting me, me being young,
An old man came courting me, saying "would you marry me,"
Maids when you're young, never wed an old man.

Chorus:
For he's got no faloo-doo-rum,
Fal-diddle-oo-doo-rum,
He's got no faloo-doo-rum, Fa-diddle-day,
He's got no faloo-doo-rum,
Lost his ding-doo-reeum,
Maids when you're young, never wed an old man.

When this old man comes to bed, hey ding doorum-da,
When this old man comes to bed, me being young,
When this old man comes to bed, he lays like he was dead,
Maids when you're young, never wed an old man.

Chorus

When this old man goes to sleep, hey ding doorum-da,
When this old man goes to sleep, me being young,
When this old man goes to sleep, out of bed I do creep,
Into the arms of a handsome young man.

Chorus

I wish this old man would die, hey ding doorum-da,
I wish this old man would die, me being young,
I wish this old man would die, I'd make the money fly,
Girls for your sake, never wed an old man.

Chorus

A young man is my delight, hey ding doorum-da,
A young man is my delight, me being young,
A young man is my delight, he'll kiss you day and night,
Maids when you're young, never wed an old man.

I THINK I'VE FOUND
THE PROBLEM MR
KELLY. IT WOULD
APPEAR YOU HAVE NO
'FALOO DOO RUM'.

the minstrel boy

Thomas Moore

A sad tale of Ireland's national emblem, the harp, which is a totally appropriate symbol for modern Ireland, because for the last eighty years the entire country has been run by pulling strings.

The minstrel boy to the war is gone
In the ranks of death you will find him.
His father's sword he has girded on
And his wild harp slung behind him.

"Land of Song!" said the warrior bard
"Though all the world betray thee,
One sword, at least, thy rights shall guard,
One faithful harp shall praise thee!"

> Making peace,
> I have found,
> is much harder
> than making war.
>
> —Gerry Adams
> *Northern Ireland Politician*
> *(b. 1948)*

The minstrel fell! But the foeman's steel
Could not bring that proud soul under.
The harp he loved ne'er spoke again
For he tore its chords asunder.

And said, "No chains shall sully thee
Thou soul of love and bravery!
Thy songs were made for the pure and free,
They shall never sound in slavery!"

YOU PLUCK MY HARP AND
I'LL PLUCK YOURS

molly malone
(cockles and mussels)

James Yorkston

The famous ditty about Molly Malone—or as she's known to Dubs since they erected a rather well-endowed statue in her honour—"The Tart with the Cart" or the slightly more complimentary "Dish with the Fish."

In Dublin's fair city where the girls are so pretty
I first set my eyes on sweet Molly Malone,
As she wheeled her wheelbarrow
Through streets broad and narrow,
Crying, "Cockles and mussels, alive, alive–o!"

Chorus:
Alive, alive-o, alive, alive-o,
Crying, "Cockles and mussels, alive, alive–o!"

COCKLES AND MUSSELS AND
TICKETS TO THE HOGAN STAND,
ALIVE ALIVE-O!!!

She was a fishmonger and sure 'twas no wonder,
For so were her mother and father before;
And they each wheeled their barrow
Through streets broad and narrow,
Crying, "Cockles and mussels, alive, alive–o!"

Chorus

She died of a fever and no one could save her,
And that was the end of sweet Molly Malone.
But her ghost wheels her barrow
Through streets broad and narrow,
Crying, "Cockles and mussels, alive, alive–o!"

Chorus

> Every man desires to live long,
> but no man would be old.

—Jonathan Swift
Author and Dean of
St. Patrick's Cathedral
(1667–1745)

the mountains of mourne

Percy French

Irish society at the time was shocked by the notion of topless women wandering the streets of London as referred to in verse two. And of course it's a complete coincidence that in the months following the release of the song, emigration of Irish males to London rose by approximately 1,000 percent!

Oh Mary, this London's a wonderful sight
With people here workin' by day and by night.
They don't sow potatoes, nor barley, nor wheat,
But there's gangs of them diggin' for gold in the street.
At least when I asked them that's what I was told,
So I just took a hand at this diggin' for gold,
But for all that I found there I might as well be,
Where the mountains of Mourne sweep down to the sea.

I believe that when writin' a wish you expressed
As to how the fine ladies in London were dressed.
Well if you'll believe me, when asked to a ball,
Faith, they don't wear no top to their dresses at all.
I've seen them myself and you could not in truth
Say if they were bound for a ball or a bath.
Don't be startin' them fashions now, Mary MacCree,
Where the mountains of Mourne sweep down to the sea.

You remember young Peter O'Loughlin of course.
Well now he is here at the head of the Force.
I met him today, I was crossing the Strand,
And he stopped the whole street with a wave of his hand.
And there we stood talking of days that are gone
While the whole population of London looked on;
But for all these great powers, he's wishful, like me
To be back where the dark Mourne sweeps down to the sea.

There's beautiful girls here, oh never you mind,
With beautiful shapes Nature never designed.
And lovely complexions, all roses and cream,
But let me remark with regard to the same,
That if that those roses you venture to sip,
The colours might all come away on your lip.
So I'll wait for the wild rose that's waitin' for me
In the place where the dark Mourne sweeps down to the sea.

WHY DO I KEEP THINKING
OF THE MOUNTAINS
OF MOURNE?

a nation once again

Thomas Davis

Ah, this rousing ballad stirs up many a memory of childhood for Irishmen everywhere. The bleeding thing was battered into you in school by the fanatically republican Christian Brothers and when you hear it nowadays it certainly makes you want to rise up, grab them by their clerical collars and beat the living bejaysus out of them.

When boyhood's fire was in my blood
I read of ancient freemen,
For Greece and Rome who bravely stood,
Three hundred men and three men;
And then I prayed I yet might see
Our fetters rent in twain,
And Ireland, long a province, be
A nation once again!

Chorus:
A nation once again,
A nation once again,
And Ireland, long a province, be
A nation once again!

And from that time, through wildest woe,
That hope has shone a far light,
Nor could love's brightest summer glow
Outshine that solemn starlight;

It seemed to watch above my head
In forum, field and fane,
Its angel voice sang round my bed,
A nation once again!

Chorus

SING IT, YE
LITTLE FECKERS!!
A NATION ONCE
AGAIN!! ... A NATION
ONCE AGAIN !!...

It whispered, too, that freedom's ark
And service high and holy,
Would be profaned by feelings dark
And passions vain or lowly;
For freedom comes from God's right hand,
And needs a Godly train;
And righteous men must make our land
A nation once again!

Chorus

So as I grew from boy to man,
I bent me to that bidding,
My spirit of each selfish plan
And cruel passion ridding;
For thus I hoped some day to aid,
Oh, can such hope be vain?
When my dear country shall be made
A nation once again!

Chorus

old maid in the garret

Traditional

A pity we can't introduce the oul' one in this little ditty to some of the lonely male hearts who populate so many other Irish ballads. Because this babe is positively gagging for it.

I have often heard it said from my father and my mother,
That going to a weddin' is the makings of another.
And if this be so then I'll go without a biddin',
Oh it's kind providence won't you send me to a weddin'.

Chorus:
And it's oh dear me! How will it be,
If I die an old maid in the garret?

Now there's my sister Jean, she's not handsome or goodlookin',
Scarcely sixteen, and a fella she was courtin'.
Now she's twenty-four, with a son and a daughter,
Here am I at forty-five and I've never had an offer!

Chorus

I can cook and I can sew, I can keep the house right tidy,
Rise up in the morning and get the breakfast ready.
But there's nothing in this wide world would make me so cheery
As a wee fat man who would call me his own dearie!

Chorus

So come landsman, come townsman, come tinker or come tailor,
Come fiddler or come dancer, come ploughman or come sailor.
Come rich man, come poor man, come fool or come witty,
Come any man at all who would marry me for pity.

Chorus

Oh well I'm away home, for there's nobody heedin',
There's nobody heedin' to poor Annie's pleadin'.
And I'm away home to me own wee-bit garret,
If I can't get a man, then I'll surely get a parrot.

Chorus

Raggle taggle Gypsy

Traditional

This is the one where everyone knows the tune, but only one die-hard knows all the lyrics and everyone else joins in irritatingly on the last three words of each verse.

There were three gypsies a-come to my door,
And downstairs ran this lady, O!
One sang high and another sang low,
And the other sang bonny, bonny, Biscayo!

Then she pulled off her silk finished gown
And put on hose of leather, O!
The ragged ragged rags about our door,
She's gone with the raggle taggle gypsy, O!

It was late last night when my lord came home,
Enquiring for his lady, O!
The servants said, on every hand,
She's gone with the raggle taggle gypsy, O!

Oh, saddle me my milk-white steed,
Go and fetch me my pony, O!
That I may ride and seek my bride,
Who is gone with the raggle taggle gypsy, O!

Oh, he rode high and he rode low,
He rode through the wood and copses, O,
Until he came to an open field,
And there he espied his lady, O!

What makes you leave your house and land?
What makes you leave your money, O?
What makes you leave your new wedded lord
To go with the raggle taggle gypsy, O?

What care I for my house and my land?
What care I for my money, O?
What care I for my new wedded lord?
I'm off with the raggle taggle gypsy, O!

Last night you slept on a goose-feather bed,
With the sheet turned down so bravely, O!
And tonight you'll sleep in a cold open field,
Along with the raggle taggle gypsy, O!

What care I for a goose-feather bed?
With the sheet turned down so bravely, O!
For tonight I shall sleep in a cold open field,
Along with the raggle taggle gypsy, O!

the rocky road to dublin

Traditional

Down the years there have been many interpretations (and versions) of the final, emotive cry which concludes each verse—"Whack follol de rah!" Some say its etymology lies deep in Irish pre-history, others that it's a corruption of an old Celtic war cry, and still others believe that the man who penned it was simply pissed as a newt.

In the merry month of June, when first from home I started,
And left the girls alone, sad and broken-hearted.
Shook hands with father dear, kissed my darling mother,
Drank a pint of beer, my grief and tears to smother;
Then off to reap the corn, and leave where I was born,
I cut a stout blackthorn to banish ghost and goblin;
With a pair of brand new brogues I rattled o'er the bogs,
Sure I frightened all the dogs on the rocky road to Dublin.

Chorus:
One, two, three, four, five,
Hunt the hare and turn her down the rocky road
And all the way to Dublin, whack follol de rah!

In Mullingar that night I rested limbs so weary,
Started by daylight with spirits light and airy;
Took a drop of the pure to keep me heart from sinking,
That's always an Irishman's cure whene'er he's on for drinking,

To see the lassies smile, laughing all the while
At my comical style, set my heart a-bubblin';
They asked if I was hired, the wages I required,
Until I was almost tired of the rocky road to Dublin.

Chorus

In Dublin next arrived, I thought It was a pity
To be soon deprived of a view of that fine city;
'Twas then I took a stroll all among the quality,
My bundle then was stole in a neat locality.
Something crossed my mind, thinks I, I'll look behind,
No bundle could I find upon my stick a-wobblin';
Inquiring for the rogue, they said my Connaught brogue,
Wasn't much in vogue on the rocky road to Dublin.

A coachman raised his hand as if myself was wantin',
I went up to a stand full of cars for jauntin'.
Step up, my boy! says he; ah! that I will with pleasure,
And to the Strawberry Beds I'll drive you at your leisure,
A strawberry bed, says I. Faith! that would be too high,
On one of straw I'll lie, and the berries won't be troublin'.
He drove me out so far, upon an outside car.
Faith! such a jolting never were, on the rocky road to Dublin.

Chorus

I soon got out of that, my spirits never failing,
I landed on the quay just as the ship was sailing.
The captain at me roared, swore that no room had he,
But when I leapt on board, a cabin found for Paddy.
Down among the pigs I played with rummy rigs,
Danced some hearty jigs, with the water round me bubblin'.
But when off Holyhead I wished that I was dead,
Or safely put in bed on the rocky road to Dublin.

Chorus

The boys in Liverpool, when in the dock I landed,
Called myself a fool, I could no longer stand it,
My blood began to boil, my temper I was losin'.
And poor old Erin's Isle they all began abusin'
"Hurrah! my boys," says I, my shillelagh I let fly,
Some Galway boys were by, they saw I was a hobblin'.
Then, with a loud hurray! they joined me in the fray,
And then we cleared the way for the rocky road to Dublin.

> "Ireland unfree shall never be at peace."
>
> —Patrick Henry Pearse
> *Patriot and Poet*
> *(1879–1916)*

the ROSe Of tRalee

William P. Mulchinock

It's cringe-inducing, tacky and utterly tasteless. The contest, that is, not the song. That's pretty good. There go my free passes for this year's show. Darn!

The pale moon was rising above the green mountain,
The sun was declining beneath the blue sea;
When I strayed with my love to the pure crystal fountain,
That stands in the beautiful vale of Tralee.

Chorus:
She was lovely and fair as the rose of the summer,
Yet 'twas not her beauty alone that won me.
Oh no, 'twas the truth in her eyes ever dawning,
That made me love Mary, the Rose of Tralee.

IF I WIN I WOULD LIKE TO DEDICATE
MY TIME TO HELPING LITTLE
CHILDREN AND SAVING THE WHALES

The cool shades of evening their mantle were spreading,
And Mary, all smiling, sat listening to me;
The moon through the valley her pale rays was shedding,
When I won the heart of the Rose of Tralee.

Chorus

On the far fields of India, mid war's bloody thunder,
Her voice was a solace and comfort to me;
But the cold hand of death has now torn us asunder,
I'm lonely tonight for my Rose of Tralee.

Chorus

> In matters of grave importance,
> style, not sincerity,
> is the vital thing.
>
> —Oscar Wilde
> *Poet and Dramatist*
> *(1854–1900)*

spancil hill

Michael Considine

**Another chap yearning for his lost homeland and his
lost love. There are so many of these it's a wonder there's
anyone left in the bleeding country at all. At all, at all,
at all, at all.**

Last night as I lay dreaming of pleasant days gone by,
My mind being bent on rambling to Ireland I did fly.
I stepped on board a vision and sailed out with the wind,
Till I gladly came to anchor at the cross of Spancil Hill.

It being the twenty third of June, the day before the fair,
Sure Ireland's sons and daughters, they all assembled there.
The young, the old, the brave and the bold, their
    duties to fulfil,
There were jovial conversations at the fair of Spancil Hill.

I called to see my neighbours, to hear what they might say,
The old were getting feeble and the young ones turning grey.
I met with tailor Quigley, he's as brave as ever still,
Sure he always made my breeches when I lived in Spancil Hill.

I paid a flying visit to my first and only love,
She's as pure as any lily, and as gentle as a dove.
She threw her arms around me, saying "Johnny I love you still,"
She is Mack the Ranger's daughter, the pride of Spancil Hill.

I thought I stooped to kiss her, as I did in days of yore,
Says she, "Johnny you're only joking, as you often were before."
The cock crew on the roost again, he crew both loud and shrill,
And I awoke in California, far, far from Spancil Hill.

But when my vision faded, the tears came in my eye,
In hope to see that dear old spot, some day before I die.
May the joyous King of Angels his choicest blessings spill,
On that glorious spot of nature, the cross of Spancil Hill.

the spanish lady

Traditional

Ah yes! A song with a bit of everything—an exotic foreign beauty, a man with a foot fetish, and a chorus comprised of words from no known dialect on earth. What more could you ask for?

As I went out through Dublin City
At the hour of twelve at night,
Who should I see but a Spanish lady
Washing her feet by candle light.
First she washed them, then she dried them,
Over a fire of amber coals,
In all my life I ne'er did see
A maid so sweet about the soles.

Chorus:
Whack fol the toora loora laddy,
Whack fol the toora loora lay.
Whack fol the toora loora laddy,
Whack fol the toora loora lay.

I stopped to look but the watchman passed,
Says he, "Young fellow, the night is late,
Along with you home or I will wrestle you
Straight away through the Bridewell gate."
I threw a look to the Spanish lady,
Hot as the fire of amber coals,
In all my life I ne'er did see
A maid so sweet about the soles.

Chorus

As I walked back through Dublin City
As the dawn of day was o'er,
Who should I see but the Spanish lady
When I was weary and footsore.
She had a heart so filled with loving
And her love she longed to share,
In all my life I ne'er did see
A maid who had so much to spare.

Chorus

I've wandered north and I've wandered south,
By Stoneybatter and Patrick's Close,
Up and around by the Gloucester Diamond
And back by Napper Tandy's house.
Old age has laid her hands on me,
Cold as a fire of ashy coals,
But where is the lonely Spanish lady
Neat and sweet about the soles?

Chorus

As I was leaving Dublin City
On that morning sad of heart,
Lonely was I for the Spanish lady
Now that forever we must part.
But still I always will remember,
All the hours we did enjoy,
But then she left me sad at parting
Gone forever was my joy.

Chorus

the waxies' dargle

Traditional

You just can't argue with a title like that. The Waxies, if you're interested, refers to the candlemakers. And the Dargle is the river which reaches the shore of Ireland near Bray in County Wicklow. The Waxies' Dargle was their annual outing, or piss-up, in more contemporary parlance. Now there's some useless information to bore your friends with the next time you're in the pub.

Says my oul' wan to your oul' wan
Will ye come to the Waxies' Dargle?
Says your oul' wan to my oul' wan,
Sure I haven't got a farthing.
I've just been down to Monto town
To see uncle McArdle
But he wouldn't lend me half a crown
To go to the Waxies' Dargle.

Chorus:
What are ye having, will ye have a pint?
Yes, I'll have a pint with you, sir,
And if one of us doesn't order soon
We'll be thrown out of the boozer.

Says my oul' wan to your oul' wan
Will ye come to the Galway races?
Says your oul' wan to my oul' wan,
With the price of my oul' lad's braces.

I went down to Capel Street
To the pawn shop moneylenders,
But they wouldn't give me a couple of bob
On my oul' lad's red suspenders.

Chorus

Says my oul' wan to your oul' wan
We have no beef or mutton,
But if we go down to Monto town
We might get a drink for nothin'.
Here's a piece of good advice
I got from an oul' fishmonger:
When food is scarce and you see the hearse
You'll know you've died of hunger.

Chorus

> **What is mind? No matter.
> What is matter? Never mind.**
>
> —George Berkeley
> *Philosopher*
> *(1685–1753)*

whiskey in the jar

Traditional

For anybody under forty who is contemplating singing this at a hooley, a word of warning: when it was originally written, there was no such thing as an electric air guitar solo.

As I was going over the Cork and Kerry mountains
I met with Captain Farrell and his money he was counting.
I first produced my pistol and then produced my rapier,
Saying, "Stand and deliver, for you are a bold deceiver."

Chorus:
Musha ring dumma do dumma da,
Whack for my daddy-o,
Whack for my daddy-o,
There's whiskey in the jar.

I counted out his money, and it made a pretty penny.
I put it in my pocket and I brought it home to Jenny.
She sighed and she swore that she never would deceive me,
But the devil take the women, for they never can be easy.

Chorus

I went into my chamber all for to take a slumber,
I dreamt of gold and jewels and for sure it was no wonder.
But Jenny took my charges and she filled them up with water,
And sent for Captain Farrell to be ready for the slaughter.

Chorus

'Twas early in the morning before I rose to travel,
up comes a band of foot men and likewise Captain Farrell.
I first produced my pistol, for she stole away my rapier,
But I couldn't shoot the water so a prisoner I was taken.

Chorus

If anyone can aid me, it's my brother in the army,
If I can find his station in Cork or in Killarney.
And if he'll come and save me, we'll go roving near Kilkenny,
And I swear he'll treat me better than my own
   dear darling Jenny.

Chorus

Now some men take delight in the carriages a-rolling,
And others take delight in the hurling and the bowling.
But I take delight in the juice of the barley,
And courting pretty fair maids in the morning bright and early.

wild colonial Boy

Traditional

**We sent the Aussies the wild colonial boy to pillage
and plunder their warm and fair land. They sent us
Neighbours in revenge. The bastards!**

There was a wild colonial boy, Jack Duggan was his name,
He was born and raised in Ireland, in a place called Castlemaine;
He was his father's only son, his mother's pride and joy,
And dearly did his parents love the wild colonial boy.

At the early age of sixteen years he left his native home,
And to Australia's sunny shore he was inclined to roam;
He robbed the rich, he helped the poor, he shot James MacEvoy,
A terror to Australia was the wild colonial boy.

One morning on the prairie, as Jack he rode along,
A-listening to the mocking bird, a-singing a cheerful song;
Up stepped a band of troopers: Kelly, Davis and Fitzroy,
They all set out to capture him, the wild colonial boy.

Surrender now, Jack Duggan, for you see we're three to one,
Surrender in the King's high name, you are a plundering son;
Jack drew two pistols from his belt, he proudly
    waved them high,
"I'll fight, but not surrender," said the wild colonial boy.

He fired a shot at Kelly, which brought him to the ground,
And turning round to Davis, he received a fatal wound;
A bullet pierced his proud young heart, from
    the pistol of Fitzroy,
And that was how they captured him,
    the wild colonial boy.

> *All publicity is good,*
> *except an obituary notice.*
> —Brendan Behan
> *Playwright*
> *(1923–1964)*

the wild rover

Traditional

The most popular Irish party piece in the history of Irish party pieces, it's a cautionary tale of a man filled with guilt for a wild life spent consuming vast quantities of whiskey and beer, usually sung by some gobshite who's just consumed vast quantities of whiskey and beer.

I've been a wild rover for many's the year,
And I've spent all my money on whiskey and beer,
But now I'm returning with gold in great store,
And I never will play the wild rover no more.

Chorus:
And it's no, nay, never,
No, nay, never no more,
Will I play the wild rover,
No, never no more.

I went into an alehouse I used to frequent,
And I told the landlady my money was spent.
I asked her for credit, she answered me "nay,
Such custom as yours I could have any day."

Chorus

I took from my pockets ten sovereigns bright,
And the landlady's eyes opened wide with delight.
She says "I have whiskey and wines of the best,
And the words that I spoke sure were only in jest."

Chorus

I'll go home to my parents, confess what I've done,
And I'll ask them to pardon their prodigal son.
And when they've caressed me as oft times before,
I never will play the wild rover no more.

Chorus

four

luvely
recipes

yer ma useta
make when you were
a little gurrier

A SHORT NOTE FROM THE KITCHENS

ALL OF THE RECIPES IN THIS CHAPTER
HAVE BEEN FULLY TESTED
AND NONE HAVE BEEN FOUND TO BE RADIOACTIVE.

horse it into ye!

It may come as a surprise to some that Ireland is renowned the world over for the great wealth of its cuisine. Sorry, that should have read "the great wealth of its politicians." But really, in Ireland you can't beat eating. Well, okay, you can. There's drinking. And of course there's sex. So it's just as well this section of the book combines all three in a hearty Irish stew.

Naturally, you'll find all those famed dishes of the Emerald Isle, like Dublin Coddle, Boxty, Irish Stew, Soda Fruit Bread, and so on. So, if you find yourself feeling like you could ate a baby's arse through the bars of a cot, get back to your kitchen and read this chapter.

And, if you blend in these uniquely Irish recipes with some of Ireland's favorite ingredients of politics, religion, and cynicism, this section of the book is guaranteed to satisfy almost any appetite.

So bon appetit! Or as they say in Ballybunion, get that into yer gob ye dirty little bowsie ye!

main courses

ᓍᑌᗷᒪᓰᘉ ᒪᓍᕲᕲᒪᘓ

Dublin Coddle is a mouthwatering dish that's likely to bring back many a memory to Irish people—like unemployment, having no central heating, the Christian Brothers beating the crap out of you, etc.

INGREDIENTS
2 lb (1kg) pork sausages, cut into bite-sized pieces
½ lb (250g) streaky bacon, cut into 1-inch (2cm) pieces
1¾ pt (1ltr) boiling water
2 large onions, peeled and coarsely chopped
2 lb (1kg) potatoes, peeled and thickly sliced
3 tbsp chopped parsley
salt and pepper to taste
large glass of cider

YER A LITTLE FECKER MURPHY. WHAT ARE YEH?

METHOD

- Place the sausages and bacon in the boiling water and cook for 5 minutes.
- Drain, but reserve the liquid. (Now remember this—don't go draining the thing over the bloody sink!)
- Put the meats into a large saucepan along with the onions, potatoes, and parsley.
- Add enough of the reserved liquid and some cider to just cover the contents.
- Cover the pot and simmer gently for about one hour, or until the liquid is reduced by half and all the ingredients are cooked. (Don't let them go mushy or, like Brian Boru, you'll be history.)
- Season with salt and pepper.

Serves 4–6

" He was a bold man
that first eat an oyster. "

—Jonathan Swift
Author and Dean of St. Patrick's Cathedral
(1667–1745)

beef anD GuInness casseRole

This is consumed by people all over Ireland as a lunchtime treat, at dinner, or even for supper. Beef is also widely consumed.

INGREDIENTS
2 lb (1kg) round or rump steak, cubed
2 oz (50g) plain flour
seasoned sunflower oil
2 medium potatoes, peeled and cubed
2 medium onions, thickly sliced
3 cloves garlic, thinly sliced
2 large carrots, sliced
1 tsp parsley, finely chopped
1 tsp thyme
1 bay leaf
salt and black pepper to taste
½ pt (300ml) beef stock (use a stock cube)
1 pt (600ml) Guinness

METHOD

- Coat the cubes of beef in flour.
- Brown the beef in oil in a pan, then transfer to a large saucepan. (You may need to do this in batches.)
- Lightly fry onions and garlic in the meat residue in the pan, then add to the beef.
- Now add potatoes, carrots, parsley, thyme, and bay leaf.
- Season with salt and pepper.
- Pour the Guinness and stock over the meat and vegetables and bring to a boil.
- Reduce heat and simmer for 30 minutes.
- Using a slotted spoon, lift meat, onions, potatoes, and carrots from pot to a heated serving dish.
- Over a high heat, reduce the gravy to half the original volume. Pour gravy over meat and serve.

Serves 4–6

> There are so few who can grow old with grace.

—Sir Richard Steele
Essayist and Playwright
(1672–1729)

sausage and bacon pie

First of all, relax. This one's a complete doddle.
And after you've eaten all that bacon and sausage,
you should definitely feel like a pig.

INGREDIENTS
1 lb (500g) Irish streaky bacon
1 lb (500g) Irish sausages
4 large potatoes, peeled and thinly sliced
2 oz (50g) mushrooms, thickly sliced
16 fl oz (500ml) vegetable stock
2 tbsp sunflower oil
pinch of thyme
1 medium onion, diced
a few sprigs of parsley, chopped
salt and pepper to taste

> I love everything that's old:
> old friends, old times,
> old manners, old books,
> old wine.
>
> —Oliver Goldsmith
> *Poet and Writer*
> *(1728–1774)*

METHOD

- Heat the oil in a pan, brown sausages and sauté (posh word for "fry lightly") the bacon (posh word for "rashers").
- Toss the potatoes (semi-posh word for "spuds") with the herbs and onion and season with salt and pepper.
- Put half the potato mix in an ovenproof dish.
- Place sausages, bacon, and mushrooms on top, then cover these with the remaining potato mix.
- Pour over stock until they are just covered (easiest way to make stock is to use a stock cube).
- Cook in pre-heated oven at 425°F (220°C) for 20 minutes, until the potatoes are lightly browned.
- Reduce temperature to 335°F (170°C) and cook for another 30 minutes, pressing down the potatoes occasionally during cooking.
- Garnish with chopped parsley and serve.

Serves 6

Black pudding and vegetable casserole

The only question here is what you're going to do with the other three quarters of the cabbage that you don't actually use. Personally, I couldn't give a toss.

INGREDIENTS
2 Irish black puddings, skinned and sliced
2 large potatoes, peeled and diced
2 carrots, peeled and sliced
1 leek, sliced
4 small onions, cut into wedges
¼ small white cabbage, shredded
1 can red kidney beans, drained and rinsed
1 chicken stock cube
salt and pepper to taste
2 tbsp sunflower oil

> "There are no persons capable of stooping so low as those who desire to rise in the world."
>
> —Marguerite Blessington
> *Countess of Blessington*
> *(1789–1849)*

METHOD

- Chuck the onions, carrots, potatoes, and leek into a large saucepan with 1½ pt (0.75ltr) of boiling water.
- Add stock cube. (Don't forget to crumble it, ye big eejit!)
- Cover and cook for about 25 minutes until the vegetables are almost tender.
- Add the cabbage and the kidney beans and cook for another 5 minutes. (Kidney beans were not as widely available in Kerry in the 1950s as is commonly thought, so some of the oul' wans used to use a tin of baked beans, sauce and all!)
- Fry the slices of black pudding in oil until they are crispy on the outside.
- Gently fold into vegetables and simmer for 10 minutes.
- Season and serve hot with fresh bread rolls.

Serves 4

GET YER THREEQUARTA' CABBAGES
TWENTY FIVE PER CENT OFFA
THE THREEQUARTA' CABBAGES!!!

irish stew

Many of Ireland's best known politicians and church leaders attribute their health and long life to regular helpings of this healthy, tasty dish. But don't let that put you off.

INGREDIENTS
1 lb (500g) stewing lamb, cubed
1 lb (500g) carrots, sliced
1 lb (500g) onions, cut into wedges
1 lb (500g) large potatoes, peeled and quartered
½ lb (250g) parsnips, thickly sliced
salt and pepper
pinch of thyme

IT'S MADE ME WHAT I AM TODAY

WHAT? A VEGETABLE?

METHOD

- Put a layer of dead animal (meat) into a large saucepan.
- Cover with a layer of carrot, onion, parsnip, and potatoes and sprinkle with thyme and seasoning.
- Repeat the process, ending with a layer of potatoes.
- Add sufficient cold water to cover.
- Bring slowly to the boil and simmer for 1 hour, which is just enough time to nip down to the pub for a quick one.
- Add more seasoning to taste, if required.

Serves 4

> Ambition often puts men upon doing the meanest offices; so climbing is performed in the same position with creeping.

—Jonathan Swift
Author and Dean of St. Patrick's Cathedral
(1667–1745)

cod cobbler

Every time my Auntie Brigid served this to my Uncle Padraig, he used to mutter "Go n-ithe an cat thú is go n-ithe an diabhal an cat," which I finally discovered means "May the cat eat you, and may the cat be eaten by the devil." Maybe she was using too much salt. Or maybe he was just nuts.

INGREDIENTS
1½ lb (750g) fillets of cod, skinned

For the cheese sauce:
2 oz (60g) butter
2 oz (50g) plain flour
½ pt (300ml) milk
4 oz (100 g) grated cheddar cheese

For the scone topping:
8 oz (200g) self-raising flour
2 oz (50g) grated cheddar cheese
2 oz (50g) butter
pinch of salt
yolk of 1 egg
milk as needed

THERE'S SOMETHING FISHY ABOUT THIS ONE.

METHOD

- Lay the cod fillets in a round ovenproof dish.
- For the sauce: Melt butter in small saucepan. Remove from heat. Stir in the flour until the mixture is dry and sandy. Gradually add the milk, stirring continuously. Return to heat, continue stirring and bring to a boil. Stir in cheese.
- Pour the cheese sauce over the fish.
- Put the flour for the scones in a bowl and rub in the butter. Add pinch of salt and grated cheese.
- Stir in the egg yolk and enough milk to make a workable dough.
- Roll out to a thickness of ½ inch (1cm) and cut into small rounds with a cutter or tumbler.
- Lay the rounds on top of the cheese sauce so that they just about cover the surface.
- Glaze them with a little milk, sprinkle on some grated cheese and bake at 400°F (200°C) for 25–30 minutes or until the scones are golden brown.

Serves 4

potato, cabbage, and bacon casserole

Is there any traditional Irish dish that doesn't feature feckin' potatoes, I hear you ask. Well, the answer is yeah, of course there is—Irish coffee.

INGREDIENTS
½ lb (250g) green cabbage, shredded
1 large onion, coarsely chopped
¼ lb (125g) bacon piece
1 tbsp chopped parsley
½ tsp thyme
salt and pepper
1 lb (500g) potatoes, peeled and thinly sliced
½ pt (300ml) chicken stock
2 oz (50g) grated cheddar cheese

EAT YOUR SPUDS
AND YOU'LL GROW
UP BIG AND
STRONG LIKE ME

METHOD

- Cut the bacon into ½-inch (1cm) cubes.
- In an ovenproof casserole dish, spread a layer of cabbage and onion and cover with bacon. Sprinkle with parsley, thyme, and salt and pepper. Arrange a layer of sliced potatoes on top.
- Repeat the process, ending with potatoes.
- Pour chicken stock over layers.
- Cover and bake in a preheated oven at 400°F (200°C) for 45 minutes.
- Uncover. Sprinkle with the grated cheese and cook for a further 15 minutes, until top is brown.

Serves 4

" The more I see
of the moneyed classes,
the more I understand
the guillotine. "
—George Bernard Shaw
Dramatist
(1856–1950)

chicken, bacon, and leek pie

Guaranteed to warm the cockles of your heart. Not to mention the cockles of your various other bodily parts.

INGREDIENTS

4 lean chicken breasts, diced
8 slices streaky bacon, grilled and chopped
4 leeks, white part only, thinly sliced
2 tbsp parsley, finely chopped
1 tsp dried sage
1 tsp salt
½ tsp freshly ground black pepper
1 lb (500g) wholewheat flour
½ lb (250g) lard
¼ c (50ml) milk
1 egg, beaten
3 tbsp water

METHOD

- In a mixing bowl, combine the chicken, bacon, leeks, parsley, sage, and half the black pepper.
- In a separate bowl mix together the flour with the salt and remaining black pepper.
- In a saucepan heat the lard, milk, and water until the lard melts.
- Make a hole in the centre of the flour mixture and pour in the liquid. Mix to a dough.
- Roll out two thirds of the dough lightly and use it to line an ovenproof dish or pie mould.
- Fill with the chicken mixture and cover with the remaining pastry.
- Brush the top with the beaten egg.
- Bake at 275°F (140°C) for 2 hours.
- Serve hot or cold.

Serves 6

THOUGHT MY COCKLES
WERE ABOUT TO DROP OFF.

steak and guinness pie

The length of time waiting for this dish to cook (two and a half hours), combined with the absence of a TV in the 1950s/1960s, goes some way to explaining why Irish families used to be so large.

INGREDIENTS
2 lb (1kg) round steak, cubed and rolled in seasoned flour
1 tbsp plain flour
1 tsp brown sugar
2 large onions, peeled and finely chopped
2 oz (50g) button mushrooms
½ pt (300ml) Guinness
8 slices of streaky bacon
chopped parsley
1 pack frozen shortcrust pastry, thawed

METHOD

- Grill the bacon, cut into pieces, and place in a saucepan with the steak.
- Fry onions and mushrooms until golden and add to the saucepan.
- Add the sugar and the Guinness. Cover and simmer over a low heat for 2 hours.
- Stir occasionally, adding a little more Guinness if gravy thickens too much.
- Line a deep pie dish with half the pastry and bake at 425°F (220°C) for 10 minutes.
- Add the Guinness and beef mixture from the saucepan and cover with the top layer of pastry.
- Bake for 10 more minutes, or until brown.

Serves 4

corneð beef anð cabbage

Tip 1: Soak your joint overnight in several changes of water to remove excess salt.
Tip 2: If you are a student, in this context a joint is a piece of meat.

INGREDIENTS
3 lb (1.5kg) joint of corned beef
1 large green cabbage, cut into wedges
2 large onions, quartered
4 medium carrots, thickly sliced
1 tsp freshly ground black pepper
1 bay leaf
1 clove garlic

> A great artist is always
> before his time or behind it.
>
> —George Moore
> *Writer*
> *(1852–1933)*

METHOD

- Pour off the water in which the joint has been soaking and cover the corned beef with fresh cold water. Bring to a boil in a large saucepan.
- Skim off any surface scum (sorry, there's no nicer word I can think of) and add the bay leaf, pepper, and garlic.
- Simmer gently for 2 hours, or until the beef is tender.
- Add the carrots and onions and simmer for an additional 15 minutes.
- Add the cabbage and cook for another 15 minutes.
- Serve the corned beef, sliced across the grain, on a platter surrounded by the vegetables and with a side dish of Champ (see recipe on p. 262).

Serves 4

CRUBEENS

If you're a vegetarian who's always thought that crubeens was some form of tasty, nutritious bean dish, boy are you in for a shock.

INGREDIENTS
The hind trotters of 4 unfortunate pigs (hind ones are meatier)
1 large onion, quartered
1 medium carrot, sliced
1 bay leaf
1 tbsp parsley, chopped
1 tsp thyme
1 tsp salt
1 tsp whole black peppercorns

METHOD

- Chuck all the ingredients into a large saucepan.
- Cover with cold water, bring to a boil, and simmer for 3 hours.
- That's basically it. Remove the trotters and eat them off the bone.

None of yer fancy haute cuisine here, pal.

P.S. Discard vegetables.

Serves 2

> I've always admired the American constitution. I mean, to be able to stuff so much food into their faces in such a short time requires an incredible constitution.
>
> —Sinead Murphy
> *Irish Writer*
> *(b.1959)*

the great
irish spud

Boxty

Boxty is especially nice with bacon, sausages, fried eggs,
and black pudding. A health tip: if you eat this meal on
a regular basis you will be dead in about 3 weeks.

INGREDIENTS

½ lb (250g) raw potatoes, grated
½ lb (250g) cooked mashed potatoes
½ lb (250g) plain flour
milk
1 large egg (mugged, or if you prefer, beaten up)
salt and pepper

METHOD

- Mix grated potatoes with the cooked mashed potatoes.
- Add flour, salt, and pepper.
- Add egg to mixture with just enough milk to make a
  batter that will drop from a spoon.
- Drop by tablespoonfuls onto a hot griddle/frying pan.
- Cook over a moderate heat for 3–4 minutes on each side
  until golden brown.

Makes 8 cakes

BOXTY
VICTIM

champ

I've been told that this simple dish originated in Cavan, where people are, reputedly, careful with their pennies. A story goes that a Cavan man on his deathbed asked for one final helping of his beloved champ, only to be told by his wife that she was saving the champ for AFTER the funeral.

INGREDIENTS
4 lb (2kg) potatoes
½ lb (250g) spring onions (posh word for scallions)
½ pt (300ml) milk
1 tsp salt (or to taste)
4 oz (100g) butter

" Nothing is so hard
for those who abound in riches
as to conceive how others
can be in want. "

—Jonathan Swift
Author and Dean of St. Patrick's Cathedral
(1667–1745)

METHOD

- Boil the potatoes until cooked. (You did remember to peel them first, didn't you?)
- Simmer the scallions in milk for about 5 minutes.
- Strain potatoes and mash them.
- Add the hot milk, scallions, salt, pepper, and half the butter to the mashed potatoes and mix together.
- Serve in a nice dish with remaining knob of butter propped artistically in the centre.

Serves 4

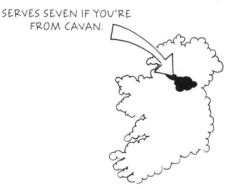

SERVES SEVEN IF YOU'RE FROM CAVAN.

spud soup

There's a woman in Borris-in-Ossory who claims that this recipe is the perfect cure for the common cold. (When taken in conjunction with a box of aspirin and a gallon of hot honey/lemon drinks, while staying in bed for three days with a box of man-size tissues.)

INGREDIENTS
2 lb (1kg) potatoes, peeled and quartered
1 large onion, finely chopped
2 oz (200g) butter
1¾ pt (1ltr) vegetable stock
½ pt (300ml) milk
1 tbsp chopped parsley
¼ tsp nutmeg
1 tsp cornflour
pinch of salt and pepper

METHOD

- Melt butter in a saucepan over a gentle heat and add the onions.
- Cover and simmer for 10 minutes.
- Add the stock, potatoes, salt, pepper, and nutmeg.
- Bring to a boil, stirring continuously.
- Reduce heat, cover, and simmer for 30 minutes until veggies soften, stirring occasionally.
- Remove from heat and put through a sieve. (If you're a lazy galoot, use a food processor, but it's just not as good. And besides, yer Ma never had any of those high-falutin' gadgets in her kitchen.)
- Now, return soup to the saucepan and stir in the milk and cornflour. (It helps to mix the cornflour into a small amount of milk first.)
- Bring to a boil, stirring continuously.
- Remove from heat. Serve with a sprinkling of parsley.

Serves 4–6

colcannon

Traditionally, this dish was served exclusively at Halloween. But nowadays, with us Irish casting aside the shackles of our past, there is a new sense of adventure and a willingness to embrace exciting new ideas. Some of us have even gone so far as to eat colcannon in April!

INGREDIENTS

1 lb (500g) kale, or green cabbage, if you're stuck
½ pt (300ml) water
1 tbsp vegetable oil
1½ lb (750g) potatoes, peeled and quartered
1 medium-sized carrot, cut into chunks
1 tbsp chopped parsley
1 medium onion, finely chopped
1 cup milk
salt and feshly ground black pepper to taste
2 oz (50g) butter, melted

METHOD

- Simmer kale (or cabbage) in the water and oil for 10 minutes.
- Drain thoroughly and chop finely.
- Boil potatoes and carrot (you can put both in the same pot), until tender.
- Put the milk and onion in a saucepan and cook lightly (the onion should still have a little bite).
- Drain the potatoes and carrot and mash together.
- Add the onion and its milk and the cooked kale to the potato/carrot mash and mix together well.
- Season with salt and pepper.
- Transfer to a warmed serving dish. Make a well in the centre and pour in the melted butter.
- Garnish with parsley.

Serves 4

BReADS, CAKes, AND DESSERTS

AH .... NO DESSERT FOR ME.
I'M SWEET ENOUGH AS IT IS.

soda fruit bread

Man cannot live by bread alone, but with soda fruit bread, now that's a different story. Oops, I'm damned for eternity.

INGREDIENTS
8 oz (200g) plain flour
1 tsp bread soda
2 oz (50g) sugar
½ lb (250g) raisins
1½ tsp baking powder
½ tsp salt
1 tsp caraway seeds (optional)
½ pt (250ml) buttermilk

METHOD
- Mix all the dry ingredients in a large bowl.
- Add buttermilk and mix well with a wooden spoon.
- Spoon mixture into a lined and greased loaf tin.
- Bake at 350°F (180°C) for 50–60 minutes.
- Remove just before it turns brown.

iRish tipsy cake

This is a brilliantly simple recipe that requires very little work and minimum intelligence. So even the guy responsible for Dublin's traffic management could probably make it.

INGREDIENTS

1 lb (500g) sponge cake (If you use a jam Swiss roll omit the next ingredient)
3 tbsp strawberry/raspberry jam
large measure of Irish whiskey
¼ pt (125ml) sherry
1 pt (500ml) custard (hot)
½ pt (250ml) whipped cream

METHOD

- Spread jam roughly over cake and then cut into small pieces.
- Place in a serving dish.
- Mix sherry and whiskey and pour over cake.
- Press down lightly with the back of a spoon.
- Pour custard over the cake and chill.
- Spoon whipped cream over top and serve.

treacle breads

My Ma never made this so I don't actually know anything about it. But I got the recipe from a Sligo girl who says her granny used to make this for her every week. And she ended up marrying a rich husband, has four kids, a huge house, a yacht, and a Porsche. Draw your own conclusions.

INGREDIENTS
2 tbsp dark treacle
⅓ pt (200ml) milk
1½ tbsp sugar
1 lb (500g) flour
½ tsp salt
1 tsp cream of tartar
1 tsp bread soda
pinch of ground ginger

DOES THIS LOOK LIKE A MAN WITH TREACLE BREAD ON HIS MIND?

METHOD

- Heat the treacle and milk together in a small saucepan, stirring continuously.
- Mix all dry ingredients together in a bowl.
- Add the milk/treacle liquid and combine until a soft dough is achieved.
- Put some flour on your hands and shape the dough into a round cake 2 inches (4cm) thick.
- Cut into farls (that's 4 quarters to you), put on a floured baking sheet and bake at 350°F (180°C) for 40 minutes.

" Never speak disrespectfully of society. Only people who can't get into it do that. "

—Oscar Wilde
Poet and Dramatist
(b.1854–1900)

irish scones

There are about as many versions of Irish scones as there are rainy days in an Irish summer, all of them claiming to be the one true version. That's all bull of course, as this is the one and only true version (according to my Ma, and I'm not going to argue with her).

INGREDIENTS
1 lb (500g) plain white flour
1 tsp baking powder
5 oz (125g) butter, softened
2 oz (50g) sugar
1 egg, beaten
⅓ pt (200ml) milk
3 oz (75g) sultana raisins (optional)

METHOD

- Mix flour and baking powder.
- Add butter and rub into the flour until the mixture resembles fine breadcrumbs.
- Stir in the sugar (add sultanas, if using).
- Add the milk and half the beaten egg, mixing well to make a soft dough.
- Turn dough onto floured board and knead lightly.
- Roll out to about 1½-inch (3cm) thickness.
- Using a cutter or tumbler, cut dough into rounds and place on a greased baking sheet.
- Brush tops of scones with remainder of beaten egg.
- Bake at 425°F (220°C) for 15 minutes or until well risen and golden brown.

Makes 8–12

irish fruit brack

Tip: If you're a student, don't forget to take the dried fruit out of the plastic bags before putting it in the bowl.

INGREDIENTS
2 lb (1kg) mixed dried fruit
6 oz (150g) brown sugar
2 tsp grated lemon rind
1 tbsp lemon juice
1 cup hot strong tea
2 measures of Irish whiskey
4 eggs, beaten
1 lb (500g) plain flour
1 tsp baking powder
1 tsp ground nutmeg

DO I GET A GRANT FOR THIS?

METHOD

- Place fruit, sugar, lemon rind and juice, tea, and whiskey into a large mixing bowl and allow to steep overnight.
- Preheat oven to 300°F (150°C).
- Brush a deep 8-inch (20cm) round cake tin with melted butter and line base and sides with greaseproof paper.
- Pour eggs onto soaked fruits and mix through.
- Sift together flour, baking powder, and spice.
- Add to fruit mixture and stir until dry ingredients are moistened.
- Spoon into prepared cake tin. Bake at 300°F (150°C) for 2 hours or until cooked. Cool slightly in tin before turning out.

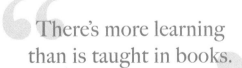

" There's more learning
than is taught in books. "

—Lady Gregory
Founder of Abbey Theater
(1852–1932)

porter cake

Porter, in case you're wondering, is not the same as stout. It is much darker and a lot weaker. But in the absence of a supply of porter, which isn't too easy to get, any stout diluted with 50 percent water will do. In the absence of stout, you may thank me for yet another invaluable excuse to go down to the pub.

INGREDIENTS
½ pt (300ml) porter or diluted stout
8 oz (225g) butter
8 oz (225g) brown sugar
2 lb (1kg) mixed dried fruit
4 oz (100g) mixed peel
1 lb (500g) plain flour (sieved)
½ tsp bread soda
1 tsp mixed spice
3 medium eggs

JUST POPPING OUT
FOR SOME INGREDIENTS...

METHOD

- Melt the butter and sugar in the porter in a saucepan.
- Add the dried fruit and mixed peel and simmer for 10 minutes.
- Allow to go cold and add the flour, bread soda, and mixed spice.
- Beat the eggs and mix in with a wooden spoon.
- Pour into a greased and lined 10-inch (25cm) cake tin and bake in a preheated oven at 325°F (160°C) for about 1 hour 40 minutes.
- Push a skewer into the centre and if it emerges clean your cake is done.
- Remove from oven and allow the cake to cool in the tin.

66 Conscience has no more to do with gallantry than it has with politics. 99

—Richard Brinsley Sheridan
Playwright
(1751–1816)

irish whiskey cake

Historians tells us that in the days before clingfilm or plastic containers, the main reason whiskey was added to foods was to act as a preservative. Yeah, right.

INGREDIENTS
8 oz (225g) raisins
6 oz (170g) brown sugar
6 oz (170g) plain flour
grated rind of 1 lemon
⅓ pt (200ml) Irish whiskey
6 oz (170g) softened butter
3 large eggs
pinch of salt
1 tsp baking powder

For the icing:
juice of 1 lemon
8 oz (225g) icing sugar
warm water

? THIS LOOKS SIMPLE ENOUGH.

METHOD

- Put raisins and grated lemon rind into a bowl with the whiskey and soak overnight.
- Preheat oven to 350°F (180°C).
- Grease a 7-inch (18cm) cake tin and line the bottom with greaseproof paper.
- Cream the butter and sugar until fluffy.
- Sift the flour, salt, and baking powder into a bowl.
- Separate the eggs. Beat the yolks into the butter and sugar, one by one, adding a spoonful of flour and beating well after each addition.
- Gradually add the whiskey and raisin mixture, alternating with the remaining flour, mixing lightly as you go.
- Finally, whisk the egg whites until stiff and fold them into the mixture with a metal spoon.
- Turn into the prepared tin and bake for about 1½ hours, or until springy to the touch. Cool for 1 hour on a wire rack.
- To make the icing, mix the lemon juice with the sieved icing sugar and just enough water to make a pouring consistency.
- Place the cake on a serving plate and spoon the icing over the cake, letting it run naturally down the sides. Allow icing to set before cutting the cake.

sherry trifle

As you know, the word "deadly" means brilliant, fantastic, great. Appropriately, there are enough calories/alcohol in each serving of this popular dessert for "deadly" to apply in every sense.

INGREDIENTS

8-inch (1x20cm) sponge cake (or trifle sponges)
1 pack raspberry/strawberry Jell-O
⅓ pt (200ml) sherry
1 tin mixed fruit, drained
1 pt (600ml) custard
1 pt of fresh whipped cream
handful of cherries
handful of mixed chopped nuts

> Among a people generally corrupt,
> liberty cannot long exist.
> —Edmund Burke
> *Lawyer, Writer, and Politician*
> *(1729–1797)*

METHOD

- Cut the sponge into fingers and arrange in the bottom and sides of a deep glass serving dish.
- Spoon mixed fruit on top.
- Prepare Jell-O as per instructions on pack but replace some of the water with the sherry.
- Pour liquid over the cake and fruit and allow the Jell-O to set in the fridge.
- Prepare custard as per instructions on pack.
- Pour cooled custard over the Jell-O.
- Before serving, pile whipped cream on top of custard.
- Arrange cherries and mixed nuts on cream.

SWEET JESUS, NO! NOT THE SHERRY TRIFLE!!!!!!

Rhubarb tart

Some famous Irish chef on TV used to say that "Patience is the key ingredient in the making of quality pastry." If like me however, you have all the patience of a starving man waiting for a turkey to roast, then simply buy the frozen stuff in the supermarket.

INGREDIENTS
½ lb (1 x 500g) pack frozen shortcrust pastry, thawed
1 cup sugar
½ cup water
2 tbsp grated lemon peel
½ tsp ground cinnamon
2 lb (1kg) fresh rhubarb, trimmed and cut diagonally
   into ½-inch (1cm) pieces

METHOD

- Preheat oven to 425°F (220°C).
- Cut ⅓ of dough for pastry cover and set aside.
- Roll out remainder of dough and line a 9-inch (23 cm) greased pie plate.
- Trim overhang and add trimmings to the set-aside dough.
- Combine sugar and water in large saucepan over low heat. Stir until sugar dissolves.
- Add lemon peel and cinnamon.
- Increase heat and bring to a boil.
- Add rhubarb and bring to a boil again.
- Reduce heat, cover and simmer until rhubarb is just beginning to soften, about 5–10 minutes.
- Remove pan from heat and cool completely.
- Using a slotted spoon, remove rhubarb from cooking liquid and arrange in circles on the pastry base.
- Strain cooking liquid into small saucepan. Boil liquid until reduced to ¼ cup.
- Cool syrup completely, then spoon over the rhubarb.
- Roll out remainder of dough.
- Wet edges of base pastry before covering with top layer. Trim edges then press down all the way around with a fork. Pierce the pastry lid several times and bake for 25–30 minutes or until golden brown.
- Serve with fresh cream.

bread pudding

Nowadays I've heard of a trendy version of this, which includes a dash of cinnamon. Oh, me granny would be turning in her grave if she was dead.

INGREDIENTS
3 eggs
½ pt (300ml) milk
1 tsp vanilla essence
2 tbsp sugar
½ loaf white bread, preferably stale
2 tbsp raisins
1 tbsp Irish whiskey

IT'S FAR FROM POXY SINMEN
YOU WERE REARED!

METHOD

- Combine eggs, milk, vanilla, and sugar in a mixing bowl.
- Cut bread into chunks or cubes.
- Add bread to egg mixture along with raisins and whiskey.
- Preheat oven to 350°F (180°C).
- Pour mixture into a greased ovenproof dish and bake for 40 minutes, or until top is golden brown.
- Serve hot with custard or whipped cream.

> **May you live
> all the days of your life.**
> —Jonathan Swift
> *Author and Dean of St. Patrick's Cathedral
> (1728–1774)*

drinks

Black velvet

Cork people will be delighted to hear that this drink works as well with Murphy's or Beamish stout as it does with Guinness. Louth folk however, may be disappointed to discover that it simply will not work with a pint of Harp.

INGREDIENTS
1 pt (600ml) Irish stout
1 pt (600ml) champagne

METHOD
* Combine chilled stout and champagne in a large glass jug.
* Stir well.
* Pour slowly into pre-chilled tall glasses.

Makes 2 pints. Surprise, surprise!

"When a true genius appears in the world, you may know him by this sign: that the dunces are all in confederacy against him."

—Jonathan Swift
Author and Dean of St. Patrick's Cathedral
(1667–1745)

hot whiskey

This simple concoction is said to be so powerful that it can actually cure a broken heart. And if that doesn't work, take ten of them in quick succession.

AH JAYSUS
YA HAVE ME
HEART BROKE
YA STUPID
WAGON!

INGREDIENTS
1 measure of Irish whiskey
1 slice lemon
4 cloves
1 tsp sugar
boiling water

METHOD
- Pour the whiskey into a glass.
- Place a spoon in the glass and add the sugar, cloves, lemon, and two measures of just-boiled water.
- Stir well, pressing on the slice of lemon to extract the juice.
- Serve immediately.

IRISH COffEE

My old man used to swear by this unique drink as a remedy for rheumatism. And the more he had of it, the more he swore.

INGREDIENTS
1 measure of Irish whiskey
1 or 2 tsp sugar (demerara, if available)
freshly made hot black coffee
2–4 tsp whipped cream

METHOD
- Warm the Irish whiskey, in a microwave if possible, for 30 seconds.
- Pour whiskey into a warmed 7-ounce Irish Coffee glass and add the sugar.
- Fill with the hot coffee to within half an inch of the top of the glass.
- Stir until the sugar is dissolved.
- Spoon the whipped cream on top of the hot coffee and serve immediately.

THIS COFFEE IS FECKIN' MANKY, GIS ANOTHER THREE...

Glossary

angelus: A devotion of the Catholic church that commemorates the Incarnation and is recited three times a day: morning, noon, and evening. At these hours a bell known as the Angelus bell is rung. In the Republic of Ireland, the Angelus bell is broadcast every evening at 6 p.m. on the TV channel RTÉ, and at noon and 6 p.m. on the radio station Radio 1.

BRIAN BORU: Also known as Brian Bórumha mac Cennétig in Gaelic, Boru became king of the province of Munster in 976. In 1002, he forced the reigning High King of Ireland to surrender his title to him. By 1011, all of the regional rulers of Ireland recognized him as their superior. The following year, the king of the province of Leinster, along with a coalition of Boru's enemies, rebelled against the High King's authority, but Boru decisively defeated this coalition in 1014 at the Battle of Clontarf, although he was killed in his tent a few days later. He is buried in Faughert in Dundalk.

CROKE PARK STADIUM/CROKER: Located in Dublin, Croke Park is the principal stadium and headquarters of the GAA, Ireland's largest sporting organization.

dáil/dáil éireann: The lower house of the *Oireachtas* (parliament) of the Republic of Ireland. The *Dáil* has the power to pass any law, and to nominate and remove the *Taoiseach*.

emmerdale: A long-running British television soap opera.

garda /gardaí: Shortened term for *Garda Síochána na hÉireann* (Guardians of the Peace of Ireland), it is the national police agency of the Republic of Ireland.

mná na héireann: In English it means "The Women of Ireland." It is the title of a famous Irish poem by Peadar O Doirnín, which has since been set to music by numerous musicians.

mp: Member of Parliament.

piles: Hemorrhoids.

rté: Acronym for *Radio Telefís Éireann*, Ireland's Public Service Broadcast station on television and radio.

taoiseach: The head of government of the Republic of Ireland and the leader of the Irish cabinet. The *Taoiseach* is appointed by the president upon the nomination of the *Dáil*.

éamon de valera ["dev"]: One of the dominant political figures in twentieth century Ireland, de Valera was a leader in the pro-Republican struggle for independence from Great Britain. He drafted Ireland's constitution, the *Bunreach na hÉireann*, and served in various public offices from 1917 to 1973, including two terms as president. He was a lifelong proponent of restoring the Irish language and ending the partition of Northern Ireland.

index

Note: Words in **boldface** indicate English terms for which there is an Irish slang equivalent in this book.